SHARING LIFE

SHARING LIFE

Official Report of the

*WCC World Consultation on
Koinonia: Sharing Life
in a World Community*

El Escorial, Spain, October 1987

Edited by
Huibert van Beek

WCC Publications, Geneva

Cover design: Edwin Hassink
ISBN 2-8254-0959-6

© 1989 WCC Publications, World Council of Churches, 150 route de Ferney,
P.O. Box 2100, 1211 Geneva 2, Switzerland

Printed in Switzerland

Table of Contents

A Hymn on Empty Hands

Fred Kaan

Music: Rieke Boerma

We come with emp-ty hands, in- tent on shar-ing our needs, our wealth but more all that we are. We meet as part-ners for each oth- er car- ing at one with peo-ple lack- ing voice or pow'r.

2. We come to learn the courage of creating
   A world of justice, hope and human worth,
   To practise skills and secrets of translating
   Our words of faith into the life of earth.

3. We would be true in sharing of resources,
   In freedom eager to receive and give —
   Be open to the Spirit's gifts and forces,
   Be broken for the world in which we live.

4. Then widen, God, our vision and vocation,
   Our joy at what in Christ you showed and gave;
   As still you share your self with all creation,
   Help us respond with all we are and have.

This text by Fred Kaan was written especially for the world consultation on ecumenical sharing of resources in El Escorial.

Introduction

The WCC-sponsored consultation at El Escorial, 24-31 October 1987, was a real meeting. Its outcome could not be predicted, and it was not, and could not be, used simply to rubber-stamp decisions which were being brought to it by the consultation's sponsors.

With these words one of the participants begins an article he wrote after the conference. Many similar statements could be quoted from what delegates reported back home. They reflect the experience of a meeting in which people took things into their own hands. Something happened at El Escorial that made it different from other ecumenical gatherings.

Yet it all began in the way these meetings are usually planned and organized. There were a few keynote speakers, testimonies were given by people from different regions and backgrounds, and there was a working document which had been prepared in a very participatory manner. Divided into carefully balanced working groups, the conference undertook the task of "formulating an ecumenical discipline for the sharing of resources" for which it had been called together. But already the opening presentations by Sithembiso Nyoni and Konrad Raiser — very different from each other in their approach but equally powerful — pointed to the need for something more fundamental, more urgent to be done. The Bible studies led by Christopher Duraisingh were a source of inspiration for a vision of sharing which is neither optional nor about resources only — a sharing of life, so that a world community of all God's people may take shape.

The conference was centred in worship, and the atmosphere of worship pervaded all its work. As the meeting unfolded, worship became the life-giving thread which wove one day into the next, around the themes of one life, one body, one people, one earth, one bread, one world, one light, one koinonia. The celebration of the daily liturgies created a mood of solidarity and community in which debate, disagreement and common decision could take place.

From the beginning women made it clear in their participation that the equal sharing of women and men in the community is the basis for all other forms of sharing. Their determined action as individuals and as a group had a decisive impact. Without them, the conference might not have generated the dynamics it did.

Halfway through the week, after the groups had done a first reporting, came the turning point. In place of the planned process of a second round of group discussion to finalize the document, a new objective came into view: to state as concisely as possible, in a short text, the basic principles of sharing — the "ground rules", as it were. The conference took hold of this challenge to speak on its own, and from then on struggled to make that happen. At the eleventh hour a radical shift in the process was required, because the participants from the South felt strongly that they could make a genuine contribution only through their regional groups. Out of all this emerged on the last day the "Guidelines for Sharing" as a covenant text, expressing the commitment of the participants and their resolve "to follow this discipline themselves and to challenge their churches and agencies to accept it". This outcome was unexpected, and for many it went beyond the expectations with which they had come to the meeting. Another result which had neither been planned nor foreseen was the affirmation of the full participation of women and youth in a special set of recommendations.

For some, the direction the conference took meant that it had given up the attempt to deal with the tedious issue of the ecumenical mechanisms for project-funding and had therefore failed to address one of its main objectives.

In fact, during the first days of the conference, the working groups did tackle this as well as many other questions. But as the meeting was grappling with its own perception of what it wanted and what it could achieve, nobody could possibly measure what had already been done. Put together, the findings of the groups do provide a wealth of material for the common discipline of which the Guidelines speak; they spell out the context and the biblical-theological convictions and suggest numerous ways for implementing the commitment to ecumenical sharing locally, regionally and globally.

For others, the conference was inevitably caught in the contradiction between the desire to change the present order and the imperative of replacing it by a radically new one. Yet the Guidelines were born out of this very awareness of the injustices of the prevailing order and of the pains and sufferings of people in all parts of the world. The participants could not do less than call for fundamental change. At the closing worship, the spirit of renewal culminated in a deep sense of personal and corporate commitment as the participants said together these simple words, taken from the Guidelines:

> *We commit ourselves:*
> ... *to a fundamentally new value system...*
> ... to the marginalized taking the centre of all decisions and actions as equal partners...
> ... to identifying with the poor and the oppressed and their organized movements...
> ... to exposing and challenging the root causes and structures of injustice...
> ... to enable people to organize themselves to realize their potentials... towards self-realization and self-determination...
> ... to mutual accountability and correction...
> ... to present to one another our needs and problems in mutual relationships...
> ... to promote the holistic mission of the church instead of disrupting and dividing by responding to one part...
> ... to overcome all barriers between different faiths and ideologies which divide the human family...
> ... to resist international mechanisms which deprive the people of the South of their resources...
> ... to shifting the power to set priorities to those who are wrongly denied both resources and power...
> ... to facilitate and promote dialogue and participation among the people of the South...
> ... to promote and strengthen ecumenical sharing at all levels: national, regional and international.

Inevitably, the Guidelines bear all the shortcomings of an uneven, unfinished, imbalanced text coming out of the hectic last hours of a large gathering.

Paradoxically that is also their strength: no church, no agency can deny that here is a genuine understanding of sharing in which justice, participation, equality and mutual trust are the basis for a common commitment of all. Those are goals which are not and should never be seen to be beyond our reach; in each situation steps can be taken towards achieving them. That is the commitment the Guidelines and the Recommendations call for. They can be heeded or ignored, but not dismissed on the ground that they are not practical.

The conference urged the WCC to take responsibility for the follow-up and to itself implement the discipline. The Central Committee has responded positively, affirming the WCC's commitment and inviting member churches to do likewise. Promoting the covenant for sharing life has thus become part of the preparation for the Assembly in 1991. Besides being a record of the meeting, this report is meant to be a resource, a "work-book" for putting into practice the discipline of the Guidelines.

For that reason it also includes some suggestions for action, drawn from experiences since the conference.

Much has been said about ecumenical sharing. Now is the time to turn our words into deeds.

HUIBERT VAN BEEK
Secretary for Ecumenical Sharing of Resources
World Council of Churches

One Life

Leader

Sisters and brothers, we have come together in this world consultation because we believe that the one God whom we serve and worship has called us to live as one family, sharing life in this one world. In the next few days, we will seek to explore what this call to a living communion, koinonia, means in our relationship to that One source of our life and to one another. We will seek to explore how our gifts, our resources and our very lives can and have to be shared; we will seek to renew our commitments and make new commitments on sharing. We would hopefully grow into a community of covenanting solidarity, accepting the disciplines of a shared life. Our own sharing of ourselves with each other at this meeting may provide the sign of our belonging to him who shared, indeed, gave his life for us all.

Let us first turn to God in repentence for the ways in which we have failed to fulfill our calling:

(congregation sits or kneels in prayer)

Voice 1

Eternal God, if in the pride of our hearts,
we have forgotten that you are the creator of the universe
the author of life, the source of all that is good,
we ask you to forgive us...

People (sing)

Nkosi, nkosi, yiba neneeba,
Krestu, krestu, yiba neneeba.
(Lord have mercy, have mercy upon us
Christ have mercy, have mercy upon us.)

Music by G. M. Kolisi

Nko–si. Nko — si, yi – ba nen — ce — ba.

Kres–tu. Kres — tu, yi – ba nen — ce — ba.

Voice 2
If the sense of security we have from material comforts has blinded our eyes to the needs of others, or made us insensitive to anguish, pain and suffering in the world, God, forgive us.

People (sing)
Nkosi, nkosi, yiba neneeba,
Krestu, krestu, yiba neneeba.

Voice 1
If we have claimed to be concerned about social justice and righteousness but have done little or nothing about them, either in our own lives or in society, God, forgive us.

People (sing)
Nkosi, nkosi, yiba neneeba,
Krestu, krestu, yiba neneeba.

Voice 2
If while criticizing the ethical compromises of others, we have made our own institutions places of comfortable life-style and centres of affluence, God, forgive us.

People (sing)
Nkosi, nkosi, yiba neneeba,
Krestu, krestu, yiba neneeba.

Voice 1
If we have failed to uphold the oneness of the human family; if we have
not believed in the communion of sharing, if we have been unwilling to
open our lives to others; if we have talked about pilgrim people but have
refused to venture out of our sheltered and privileged positions, God,
forgive us.

People (sing)
Nkosi, nkosi, yiba neneeba,
Krestu, krestu, yiba neneeba.

Voice 2
If, in the gathering of our resources, we have been unethical; if, in the
holding of our resources, we have been avaricious; if, in the sharing of
our resources, we have been power-conscious; if we have denied you by
denying others, betrayed you by betraying others, missed you by not
sharing ourselves with others, God, forgive us.

People (sing)
Nkosi, nkosi, yiba neneeba,
Krestu, krestu, yiba neneeba.

   (congregation stands)

Leader
Jesus said: "In as much as you have done to the least of them, you have
done it unto me."

Hymn
"When I need a neighbour, were you there?"

Leader (at the close of the hymn)
May the God of love pardon us;
restore us and renew us to live
as forgiven and forgiving people.

People
Amen.

Perspective of
the Grassroots Churches

SITHEMBISO NYONI

1. One of the most painful experiences in my adult life is to receive.
   Especially when something is given to me because of my compro-
   mised and vulnerable position in life.
2. One of the easiest things I have experienced is to give — especially if
   the giving is on my terms.
3. But one of the most enriching and most fulfilling experiences I have
   ever had is that of sharing.

The people who have meant a great deal to me, some of whom are in
this room, are those people with whom I have shared. The people with
whom we have shared our hopes, struggles, fears, pains, our successes,
vision of the future and — in isolated cases — some material resources;
the giving and receiving I have experienced at this level has been a
blessing to me.

Resource-sharing is an old issue in the World Council of Churches, and
debate goes back to the early seventies.

After reading the working documents of this consultation, I wondered
if I had anything new to share. I found myself with more questions than
answers and new ideas to share with you today. My first question was,
what on earth is a resource, and whose resources are we talking about?
The dictionary defines a resource as:

> wealth, supplies of goods, raw materials, etc. which a person or country has or
> can use: mineral wealth, potential water power — the productivity of the soil;
> something which can be turned to for support; that which helps in doing
> something.

My second question was, who is the grassroots church? The dictionary
says that grassroots "are ordinary people removed from political decisions
but who are affected by those decisions".

Thirdly, what is to share? The dictionary defines sharing as:

> dividing profits, costs, etc. with others; becoming part owner with others; paying part of an expense; have or use with, have in common.

At the beginning of the first church in the Acts of the Apostles, sharing meant that "no one claimed their belongings just for themselves, but everything was theirs in common" (Acts 4:32). "No one among them suffered need", resources were "distributed to each according to their need" (v.35).

Sharing is giving and receiving

As Christians from the North and South, what do we mean by resource-sharing both as practised among ourselves and beyond our national and North/South boundaries?

In talking to various sections of the Zimbabwean public, it was clear that most people see and understand resource-sharing as equivalent to the transfer of aid in terms of capital, skills, technology, knowledge and personnel from the rich to the poor nations.

According to the definitions above, sharing implies a situation of give and take in non-exploitative and non-dependent relationships. It also demands conditions of mutual trust and understanding of what resources are, what they will be used for and what kind of society people are trying to create by using any chosen resource.

Resource-sharing, therefore, is a serious theological question which calls us to examine more deeply the issues at stake. For instance, rather than looking superficially at resource-sharing as equivalent to giving and sharing aid, information and skills, we should ask the question why we still have grassroots churches in an ecumenical family of God.

Why do we have churches which are still made up of "ordinary people" removed from political, economic and thus resource-sharing decisions which affect their lives? This is a pertinent question because, according to the above meaning of resource-sharing, it is not possible to share resources among "unequals" without creating dependency and exploitative relationships.

One of the persons I talked to about the issue of resource-sharing was Senator Jacob Mudenda — our governor for Matabeleland North. His reaction was that there cannot be any resource-sharing without interaction. He went on to say that people have first to allow a two-way transfer of information between them. People have to act upon and have an effect upon each other. Such a process allows the influence to be mutual rather than one-sided. Then when material resources are shared, they give the support which is needed to create something which has emanated from some common understanding. My first reaction to his statement was that this was impossible as the politically and economically powerful will always dominate, and they feel superior as society has always told them that they are what they are because of their intelligence, their acquired wealth, skills and knowledge. But he insisted that resource-sharing has to begin with an encounter and an understanding that both parties have to give and receive.

Some aid-giving without sharing has created a beggar mentality in some poor churches. It also has unhooked the churches of the rich nations from their true responsibilities of fighting for human justice. Most of them know that what we need most is not money or technology but international economic and political justice. For instance, what the churches in South Africa need most is not necessarily cash but mainly solidarity and political action against the apartheid regime.

We therefore further need to ask the question: who defines resources, to achieve what goals, and by what means?

Do we know of any country or nation which was developed through foreign aid and projects alone? I do not know of any. A people, and thus a nation, is only able to develop when its people, including the poorest of the poor like the miners in South Africa, acquire a certain level of awareness and the ability to mobilize their inward and local resources, their capabilities to plan together, to act and to create a new society for themselves.

We, the people of the South, are calling for a new order of resource-sharing that will enable us to develop and use our own people, including women and the poorest of the poor, as a major resource; the resource-sharing which will enable us to engage in the process of awareness building and mobilize our people for development and change. First, before projects, we need the kind of resource-sharing which will enable us to build our own indigenous and local institutions through which the very poor will be able to express their political and economic needs and through which they will be able to find political and economic solutions to their present state of powerlessness, poverty and underdevelopment. This to us is development, not when the poor gather together to implement projects and then find a schooled person to report on them. Reports must be written by them through what they have become and are capable of being.

Development is therefore a political question.

In the same way, resource-sharing for development is a political question.

The so-called grassroots churches are calling us to listen to their definition of resources in terms of their struggles. They are struggling to reverse the processes of dependency, exploitation and under-development in order to live as creative beings. They are struggling to find a new and authentic meaning to life, free of poverty, hunger and outside domination. To do this, they need to have control of their own resources first, their hands and minds, their governments and their land. Mozambican churches are a case in point. Some families are starving not because they do not have enough foreign aid but because South African armed bandits are attacking, looting and displacing families. Those who resist and stay on have their land mined so that they cannot till their own land to produce food. What kind of resources does such a church need? They definitely do not need aid alone but political action against South Africa.

Most grassroots churches are in the rural countryside, sitting on and surrounded by the world's major resources: "mineral wealth, potential water power and the productivity of the soil". But most powers, including the church, are not prepared to develop these resources for the benefit of the poor; only for the remote cities and their overseas partners at the expense of the locals.

The provision of water and the productivity of the soil for the rural poor's direct use is often not a priority. Even in this day and age of global awareness of types of aid which create dependency, there has been more aid mobilized towards Africa's famine than towards development aid to prevent that famine. The media and some donor agencies highlight the famine operations more than the efforts made by Africa's rural women to prevent that famine through their humble agricultural initiatives.

The resources of food aid and money which were thus given instead of development assistance were a well-meant Christian contribution which saved lives, but they also alienated some people and diverted them from their struggles. Resource-sharing in this context requires that those who give, together with the victims of famine, must not only understand the causes of famine, but also engage in the whole struggle to try to remove them. Together, the causes of such situations should be tackled from all angles, i.e. from the local, national and international perspectives. In most cases, resource-sharing without national and international political action to correct the situation of need ends up creating long-term negative effects on the recipients.

The goal of self-reliance

Resource-sharing with grassroot churches therefore should be a process of enabling them to identify those factors which give meaning to their lives and to mobilize resources to develop them. It should also be a process of identifying that which causes pain and suffering in people's lives, what perpetuates that suffering and what prevents the suffering church from removing their pains. Christians are called to share the understanding of these pains before sharing the resources to remove them.

The ultimate goal of resource-sharing therefore must be to lead the weak to strength and self-reliance. Self-reliance here is equated with justice in which all the components which make up life and human dignity are in place. This includes economic and political self-reliance. And resources should be defined not only in terms of meeting a need but also of removing that which causes certain needs to exist. This is because there can be no meaning to life unless there is some degree of self-reliance and control over resources to support that life.

If we all agree that one of the resources is "something which can be turned to for support, and that which helps in doing something", let us put the material resources aside for a while. Putting them first has divided the church between the rich and the poor. They have been the major bases for social as well as class divisions. Let that "something" — *the resource* — be us, the human beings. Let us turn to each other first for support and *for help to look and to see the world anew*. The grassroots churches have human and spiritual resources to share. They have information, community traditions, wisdom, organization and the technology of survival.

The richer churches also have spiritual resources and other experiences to share. Let us share the *who* we are first, before we share *what* we have. This sharing of ourselves must be at both horizontal and vertical levels. For a long time, sharing has taken place between governments and top church leadership. Today there are signs of grassroots to grassroots and governments/top churches to grassroots sharing. This should be encouraged and developed. In this process, however, the rural poor have to be encouraged to be strong and to value their own resources. They also should not let go unless and until what they value is valued, expressed and appreciated by the outside. In the past, and to a very large extent now, a lot of power and information, a lot of resources are being sucked out of the grassroots churches without recognition of the source. The present relationships of resource-sharing are largely exploitative.

When we come to sharing material resources, it should be remembered that grassroots churches also have their own material resources such as potential water sources, in some cases hard cash, and land which they should be allowed to control and share rather than surrender to the powerful. The church should help such people regain their rights and control over land and its productivity, rather than give aid to the symptoms of poor people's under-development and powerlessness. Hunger, for instance, tells us a lot about what has gone wrong. It also reveals our lack of resource-sharing in the true sense of the term, based on who we are, and thus, our lack of understanding of the forces acting upon us as communities in the North and South until we are overtaken by a crisis.

If sharing is "using with or having in common" as was demonstrated by the early church, as Christians we can no longer continue to pretend that resource-sharing is taking place today.

If it were happening, there would be a better understanding of each other, and the gap between the rich and the poor would not continue to widen. The plight of the grassroots churches would not continue to get worse. The process of under-development and dependency would not continue to erode the poor at such a fast rate. The international debt question would not exist. Injustices would be fewer.

In my judgment, very few churches are sharing resources. There is presently largely the giving and receiving of aid. It also has made the giver more powerful and the receiver weaker and more dependent.

We are called first to be equals, not donors and recipients. Our first step therefore is to unite and break down the walls which divide us, be they racial, spiritual, economic, political or ideological. It is only after this that true resource-sharing can take place. As long as there exists among us an attitude of "those others and I", as long as we continue to define each other in economic and racial terms, we shall always block God's creative plan of action through resource-sharing.

The great unrecognized resource

I want to conclude by giving a concrete example and my observation as an African woman working with a grassroots movement. Daily I see resources being defined as the ruling classes of the world and as that which they control and use to consolidate their power. In the case of Africa, the reality is that the invisible basis of African survival and power is its rural women and their children. They are Africa's greatest unrecognized resource. Most African nations would have collapsed without us, the invisible and *hard-to-crush* grassroots women. This is an old and a well-known fact.

Rural women all over the developing world keep their national, social and economic fabric together and yet they are not recognized as part of national human resources. In our case, we develop the water supplies and produce the food. The little food we produce — groundnuts in West Africa and maize in Southern Africa — are grabbed from us and our children, and exchanged for foreign currency and payment of foreign debts.

Africa is going through one crisis after another, partly because it does not yet recognize, appreciate and develop some of its major resources — the land and its women who till that land. This is evident in the fact that while the process of agriculture is still in the hands of women, that is, while the land is being tilled, planted and the crops are being nursed and harvested, they are in most cases not a national concern, nor are they seen as a national resource. If land and women who till it were recognized as national resources, they would warrant national and international protection against military bandits and droughts. Famines would be avoided. Rural women's contributions only become a resource when they get into the hands of the powerful. What happens before then is often nobody's major concern. As far as most grassroots women are concerned, there is still more resource-grabbing than resource-sharing. Nobody fully understands what goes on at that level; and very little is being done to make the grassroots church a total part of international resource-sharing; and yet those women are the members of our churches who share all they have, and all they are — their time, their food and sometimes their lives for the sake of others.

How can we, people from the South, engage in a meaningful resource-sharing if we do not recognize, cherish and use the resources we have? Women do not only hold half the sky, they also invisibly produce half the world's resources, and grassroots women are the roots which also nourish these resources.

Therefore resource-sharing with grassroots churches does not begin with aid. It begins with understanding those ordinary members of God's universal church, as people who are part of God's plan for creation and renewal for a better world for all!

One Body

Leader
Christ is like a single body, which has many parts;
It is still one body, even though it is made up of different parts.
In the same way, all of us, whether Jews or Gentiles,
whether slaves or free, have been baptized into the one body
by the same Spirit,
and have all been given the one Spirit to drink.
For the body itself is not made up of only one part
but of many parts.

Voice 1
If the foot were to say, "Because I am not the hand, I don't belong to the body" that would not keep it from being a part of the body.

Voice 2
And if the ear were to say, "Because I am not an eye, I don't belong to the body" that would not keep it from being part of the body.

People
If the whole body were just an eye, how could it hear? And if it were only an ear, how could it smell?

Leader
As it is, however, every different part in the body was put just as God wanted it to be. There would not be a body if it were all only one part!

People
As it is, there are many parts but one body.

Voice 1
So then, the eye cannot say to the hand, "I don't need you."

Voice 2
Nor can the head say to the feet, "Well, I don't need you!"

Leader
On the contrary, we cannot do without the parts of the body that seem to be weaker; and those parts we think aren't worth very much are the ones which we treat with greater care; while the parts of the body which don't look very nice are treated with special modesty, which the more beautiful parts do not need.

People
God has put the body together in such a way as to give greater honour to those parts that need it.

Leader
And so there is no division in body, but all its different parts have the same concern for one another.

People
If one part of the body suffers, all the other parts suffer with it; if one part is praised, all the other parts share its happiness.

Leader
All of you are Christ's body and each one is part of it.

Towards a
Sharing Community

KONRAD RAISER

I

This consultation represents the provisional culmination of a lengthy process. Among our preparatory documents is a paper summarizing and recalling the various stages of that process, and the results achieved along the way. This simplifies my task in these introductory remarks.

I would like to draw your attention to one aspect of that paper in particular: the document rightly begins with the moratorium debate at the beginning of the seventies. That debate continues to be of central importance in the question facing us today. The proposal for a moratorium arose out of the critical re-examination of the traditional — largely bilateral and one-directional — relations in the field of mission. The proposal caused a stir but, when all was said and done, had little actual effect. The churches' interest, together with their financial commitment, had in any case by then shifted from mission to development. In that context the moratorium proposals seemed even less opportune.

The challenge to reflect critically on the conditions of ecumenical partnership was not taken up by the churches. Instead, those same years saw the rapid development and proliferation of church and ecumenical instruments to cope with the tasks of diakonia and development assistance around the world. The newly created instruments were intended to replace the old missionary bilateralism with ecumenical cooperation. But, inevitably, new centres of power and structures of dependence emerged and the one-way traffic intensified. Since then bilateral relations have once again taken the lead over against the cumbersome and complicated ecumenical procedures.

Today the problem so dramatically highlighted by the moratorium proposal is more acute than ever in the area of diakonia and development.

And, needless to say, a solution has likewise become more difficult in the meantime, in view of the tremendous expansion of the institutional and financial framework. It was in sober and self-critical recognition of this situation that the study on the ecumenical sharing of resources was started in 1976. What have we learned in these past ten years? What can we say together today?

On reading the preparatory documents I am left with a number of conflicting impressions. I shall mention only a few of them:

First impression: Everything that needs to be said has in fact long since been said. We do not need new statements of principle. Our theology is right, at least in theory. Why, then, have all these good and forceful statements of principle so far produced so few results? Is it just a practical or political problem of implementation? Have we really understood the causes of the dogged resistance to the necessary changes? Is this not perhaps where we should begin with our theological reflection?

Second impression: Many important suggestions for action and practical recommendations have been formulated. Almost without exception they are listed in the working document. Yet the latter is unlikely to inspire changes in practice. One reason for this may be the fact that the suggestions are couched in the administrative language of official ecumenical documents which tends to smooth over the contentious points. But even where the regional reports, for example, clearly state the conflicts and try to speak in concrete terms, they seem to have little more to say about the keyword "sharing" than what has already figured in recommendations and exhortations to the churches from ecumenical gatherings for many years. Is "ecumenical sharing" then simply another word for the much-demanded, but little-practised ecumenical solidarity in the struggle for justice, especially in the conflict between rich and poor? Could it be that precisely by attempting to make "sharing" into an all-encompassing tool for interpretation, we have blunted the cutting edge of the challenge to the churches?

Third impression: A year ago the world consultation on "Diakonia 2000: Called to be Neighbours" was held in Larnaca. Our preparatory documents make many references to that conference and to its report which has now been published. For an outsider, it has been difficult from the outset to see any clear distinction between the main thrusts of the two world consultations on interchurch aid and ecumenical sharing. Is there any recognizable difference between our search for credible practice in Christian diakonia (at personal, local, national and international level) and our present efforts to arrive at a common discipline of ecumenical sharing in the churches? The difficulties have not grown smaller since Larnaca. This dialogue has been going on at many levels for a very long time and was articulated in a particular way at Larnaca. How can we constructively take the dialogue further here at this meeting? If I have read the Larnaca reports correctly, the main impression taken away by many participants was: for years we have been talking *about* each other; now we have really begun to speak *to* one another, which means, to share with one another. Admittedly, little of this comes through in the official texts. The question it raises in regard to the goal of our consultation's work is this: what form would a commitment to ecumenical sharing have to take to make it clear that it has grown out of a process of "sharing" and aims to encourage the continuation of that process?

II

These questions, prompted by a reading of the preparatory documents, require us to take a closer look at the *context* of our deliberations, as indeed the revised version of the working document does. There is certainly no need for me here to reproduce the analysis of the international situation. The worldwide reality of hopeless and increasing poverty on one side, with heedless greed on the other, is too obvious to be overlooked. And equally impossible to ignore is the relentless and progressive destruction of the basis of life in both the North and the South. Since the international debt crisis, if not before, the ambiguous nature of "interdependence" has been apparent; a change in the structures has become imperative.

The causes and inter-connections have been forcefully set out in many joint ecumenical statements by church representatives from North and South. Calls to the churches have grown more urgent year by year, but they have had little effect. Our theology tells us that the churches should live as a sharing community; our global analysis, and the realization that the project of worldwide development has gone wrong, tells us that fundamental structural changes are needed — but our practice does not keep pace with our theory. The working document and the regional reports, not least those from churches in the North, speak clearly and self-critically of the churches' failure to take up the challenge they have recognized.

It will suffice here to point out some of the most obvious contradictions. For instance, we have been talking about the wholeness of the church's mission in witness and service in all six continents for a long time now. But mission and development continue as before to be separate fields; in most churches the links between them and the life of local congregations are at best tenuous, i.e. through financial contributions, and we are still far removed from partnership in the sense of genuinely reciprocal relationships. We say that ecumenical solidarity must not limit itself to the transfer of material resources, and must be expressed first and foremost in defence of the rights of the poor in their struggle for liberation and a life of human dignity. But we continue as before to be prisoners of the power of money, negotiating as between donors and receivers, and we have to acknowledge that at best the poor are there as a passive presence in our systems and structures, but not as active partners. We know from experience that a change of course leading to liberation only happens when the people concerned take their destiny into their own hands and that the obstacle is often not the lack of resources but the lack of the power to control their own resources for themselves. Yet we go on as we have always done, chasing projects and streamlining administrative procedures.

Behind these contradictions is a fundamental conflict that concerns power and powerlessness. This is obvious in the international political context, where the power struggle is becoming less and less veiled and disguised as time goes by. Yet at the same time a responsible political solution to the conflict seems to be receding further and further into the distance. Ecumenical efforts for the active exercise of Christian responsibility in the world in the past twenty years have never denied the existence of this power dichotomy, and there have been at least limited attempts to help bring about a redistribution of power (e.g. the Programme to Combat Racism). But in practice the planning and implementation of projects, consortia, country programmes, etc. have aimed rather to tame or contain this conflict than to find a productive solution or overcome it altogether. As we can see more clearly than ever today, the churches in North and South, as corporate institutions, are themselves tied into social and political structures and consequently do not stand outside this power struggle. They are part of the problem far more than a means of solving it.

Charles Elliott, the former director of Christian Aid, gives a convincing description of the assymetrical power relations in the church and in society in his book *Comfortable Compassion: Poverty, Power and the Church*.[1] In a penetrating interpretation of what the Bible says about the

---

[1] London, 1987.

powers and principalities, he comes to the conclusion that the power struggle essentially represents a spiritual challenge to the churches — in other words, it shows up their spiritual bondage. Naming the powers-that-be by name and confronting them is a task which goes beyond the political strategies needed to change systems and structures. This testimony from someone directly confronted with the contradictions of the present process of resource-sharing among the churches may be a help to us in our further deliberations.

III

It is important to keep this context in mind if we want to talk about ecumenical sharing and work at committing the churches to a common discipline of sharing. While this kind of talk reflects a self-critical awareness of the inadequacy of efforts up till now, coupled with a willingness to take new paths, we have to be equally aware of the danger that the talk of "sharing" may also serve to blur the issues. The recently affirmed theological idea of the church as a sharing community could itself mislead us into using as our explicit premise a fellowship among the churches which does not exist in fact, thus concealing the unjust structures of which the churches are also part. Moreover, the view of the church as a sharing community could lead us to focus narrowly on processes of sharing within and between churches, thereby stifling the call to practical solidarity with the poor, the majority of whom are not members of Christian communities. The other danger is that the call to ecumenical sharing could be understood principally as reinforcing the moral appeal and challenge to the churches to change their manner of acting, without penetrating right to the spiritual causes of their captivity and so to the source of liberation that leads not just to new ways of acting, but to a new life.

These dangers being recognized, however, it is also clear that the vision of ecumenical sharing offers a real opportunity for a new beginning. Then we can and must talk about the experience of the church as a community of sharing and solidarity that exists as a reality and not just as a theological programme, in both North and South; we can say that in these renewed forms of the church there has been a rediscovery of the inseparable link that binds together eucharist and diakonia, the sacrament of the altar and the sacrament of the brother and the sister, the renewal of life in worship and the sharing of life in the liturgy after the Liturgy. Within churches where this has happened, and between them, new forms of sharing have developed, going beyond the fixation on money and one-sided giving and taking. Here it can be clearly seen that sharing has to do with sharing in the life of people, in reciprocal giving and taking, and is not simply a matter of transferring material goods. Here too it can be seen that the power structures which stand in the way of a community of sharing are the same in North and South. This is why solidarity in a worldwide community is vitally essential. Lastly, it can be seen that the theology of sharing itself is not an abstract idea, but rather an important aid to intepreting our own experiences and a pointer towards the sources which can constantly renew the strength for sharing.

But the language of sharing is even more basic than any of our theological or ecclesiological concepts, for it is the people's language in an elementary sense. All people know what sharing means, whether from experience or in longing hope, and they know that fullness of life is only to be found in sharing life with one another. "Sharing" is thus a fundamental symbol of life which points to the manifestation of fully human living, and so has a wider frame of reference than a moral commandment. Sharing takes place in relationships which are truly reciprocal and free of domination, in other words, the test of sharing is ultimately the sharing of power, mutual empowerment. Admittedly, this ideal vision of "sharing" is constantly being shattered by the conditions of human existence or, to put it in theological terms, human sinfulness. But precisely because people suffer from this inherent contradiction, they experience God's sharing of himself in Jesus Christ, the life of the world, as liberation for life in a sharing community.

The simple, people's language of sharing is inexorably at odds with the language of the established structures, including church structures, which follows a different logic, i.e. ultimately the logic of power. Therefore, important as it is that the language of sharing should take us beyond the level of global structural analysis, and confront us with the realities of human life, it must not be allowed to obscure the troubling reality of the assymetrical power relationships, not least within and between the churches. This is why I personally have always had difficulty with attempts to speak of ecumenical sharing where the issue is first and foremost one of justice and injustice, defence of legitimate rights and control of power through participatory decision-making processes. The South African Kairos document addresses the same problem when it asks critical questions about talk of "reconciliation". And now we are even talking about an ecumenical "system" of sharing, as though something which is a fundamental expression of fully human living could be ever be translated into administrative procedures, however transparent.

Nevertheless, we stand by the biblically founded conviction that the church is essentially a community of sharing. But this definition of the church as koinonia, which has become central in ecumenical reflection on the church, is, first and foremost, a theological statement and should not be taken as an empirical description. The church as koinonia is founded on the participation of all members in the body of Christ who shared his life with us even to death on the cross. The sharing together, in the eucharist, in the body and blood of Christ is the origin of koinonia as a community of sharing, and not the reverse. The radical over-turning of human values in regard to wealth, status, power, etc. through the cross of Jesus Christ constantly opens the way afresh for life in sharing fellowship. The varying personal abilities and resources within the community acquire new value as charismata to be shared for the good of the community. But the realization of such koinonia is itself a gift of God, through the power of God's Spirit.

The church as koinonia is called to be a living example of an effective community of sharing, prefiguring the fellowship in the kingdom of God. But wherever the church takes form among people, it is subject to the conditions of human life. It needs structures and regulations. Hence the church is always caught up in the tension between the language of sharing and the language of the established structures. Any attempt to make the reality of koinonia, opened up by God in Jesus Christ, into an ideal system is bound to fail. We can and must strive to make the relationships between the churches with their structures and regulations just, and to ensure that the exercise of power and authority within and between church structures — especially where money is concerned — is subject to effective and transparent control. But all that will still not guarantee that genuine sharing will be brought about in practice within and between these structures. In the last analysis, only the freedom granted by the Spirit of God can help us to do that.

I would therefore plead for soberness in using the language of sharing; soberness, precisely because we know the tensions and conflicts that sharing leads to in practice. The church as koinonia, as a worldwide fellowship of solidarity sharing life together — that vision is at once a description of the origin and the goal of the church; a statement about the church as the body of Christ, in the light of its eucharistic reality and in the light of its eschatological potential. We could not talk about the church in this way unless this experience of koinonia really existed. Today we see the rediscovery of the church as a sharing community in many places. But at the same time we have to admit that, as corporate institutions, most of our churches rarely live up to that image. This tension, which has given rise to open conflict in many places, and is likely to continue to do so in future, is also the driving force behind all processes of renewal in the church. The ecumenical movement lives in this tension and is nourished by it and the vision of a community of shared life is still one of the most powerful goals of the ecumenical quest.

Relations between our churches being what they are, it is only too easy to see why there is a hope for renewal in the sense of a real community of sharing. It has inspired many efforts in recent years. Some of the regional reports also warn against asking too much of ourselves and our churches in terms of a self-commitment. We already have more than enough unfulfilled declarations of intent! On the other hand, it would be a sign of resignation and weak faith if we were simply to dismiss the churches and their agencies which are represented by many participants here at this conference, because they are not open to renewal by God's Spirit. Justified though some sharp criticism may be, we should soberly face the fact that in a great many places, it is they who stand guard and keep the way open for the renewal of real fellowship.

IV

Any process of renewal is nourished by a vision which determines the direction of whatever changes are necessary, and furnishes the criteria by which to judge the path that has been travelled. The renewal we are talking about here is never completed, indeed it cannot ever be completed, and the vision of the church as a sharing world community is not static, but changes with changing experiences and insights. In recent years, as we have tried to formulate our vision in concrete terms, we have found ourselves engaged in an intensive and sometimes heated exchange of ideas. These efforts to arrive at a concrete formulation have incorporated a new reading of biblical texts as well as the evaluation of experiences of sharing — some successful, some not — in the ecumenical fellowship. The working document summarizes these insights under a few concise headings in its central section IV. There is no need for me to repeat them in detail here. While the goals could no doubt be defined more precisely, these are nevertheless useful bricks on which to build as we seek to make koinonia as a sharing community a reality, and they provide the outline of an open vision which can guide us in taking practical steps. I shall therefore conclude with some words about possible steps towards translating our vision into practice.

In doing so it is important wherever possible to pick up the existing positive experiences and consolidate and develop them in the light of our vision. This is particularly true when it comes to surmounting the one-sided concentration on the exchange of material resources. To my mind, it has not been made clear enough in the discussion so far that the whole ecumenical movement in fact represents a rich store of experiments in sharing which have succeeded. In the last few decades, the churches of Europe and North America in particular have received an immeasurable wealth of theological and spiritual perceptions and ideas, music and songs, prayers and living testimonies from the churches of the South. What kind of Christians would we in the Northern countries be if these resources had not come our way? We have probably received far more ecumenically in terms of encouragement to credible Christian witness, necessary challenge and friendly correction than we have been able to give with all our, largely material, gifts. For the younger generation in our churches in particular, this sharing of spiritual resources has become a necessary source of strength from which they can draw in their practical attempts at ecumenical solidarity. The ecumenical movement began with people meeting each other. And this is where, even today, the most effective fellowship of sharing is to be found, even if it does not seem possible to incorporate it into a comprehensive system of sharing.

What form might the practical steps towards realizing our vision take? I would like to mention a few points which may, I hope, be useful for our work here.

1. Realism tells us that, at the macro-level, relations between churches and the agencies they support will probably never measure up to the standard of comprehensive, mutual sharing, especially where the sharing of material resources is concerned. Nevertheless, these relations ought to be clearly and recognizably different from relations between governments, business corporations, etc. They should meet the fundamental requirement of justice. For only then can they keep the way open for the renewal that will lead to a sharing community. In their relations with one another, churches do not behave like autonomous states, business partners or pressure groups. As members of the body of Christ they live in a fundamental relationship to one another which binds them in mutual obligation.

This no doubt lies behind the proposal to describe the special quality of these relations in terms of commitment to a binding discipline. In another connection, the model of a covenant is being discussed at present as a means of emphasizing the binding nature of the ecumenical fellowship of churches. Israel's covenant order is reflected in its most concentrated form in the Decalogue. Significantly, the most important commandments for the social life of the community are formulated in the negative. They do not specify positively what is to be done, but what is not to be done. The exhortation to forgo a right or renounce power (cf. the Sabbath year) as a necessary pre-condition for maintaining the community between unequal partners can also be found in other passages in the scriptural tradition. This idea could perhaps be helpful to us in formulating a common discipline of sharing. Its purpose would be the commitment to refrain from doing anything which stands in the way of realizing koinonia.

2. Rather than a long list of actions and initiatives to be positively required of the churches, a commitment of this nature could limit itself to a few basic rules designating the points at which the special quality of the relations between the churches is being infringed. These would be basic rules and not a perfect system. The rules would have to be more concrete than theological or ecclesiological principles and yet be relevant to the great diversity of different situations. They should be couched in simple terms, understandable to all church members so that no one is excluded from joining in the critical examination of relations.

By analogy with the basic rules of the Old Testament covenant order, the aim of a self-commitment of this sort should be to protect the rights of the weaker members of the community and control the exercise of power. The areas for which rules would have to be made in this mutual commitment would include:

— respect for the self-reliance of all partners; self-reliance and equal rights are fundamental conditions in any sharing;
— involvement of all partners on an equal footing in decisions concerning relations;
— rules for giving and receiving, especially in the matter of directives as to the use of the resources offered;
— the scope of mutual accountability;
— one-sided or joint fixing of mandates and evaluation criteria.

These examples of aspects of relations that require some such common rules are principally concerned with the exchange of material resources.

They should, however, be extended to include in particular the ecumenical exchange of personnel.

3. Sharing in the fullest sense takes place in meetings and exchanges between people and only secondarily in the relations between institutions. Thus the attempt to formulate a common commitment in the form of a few simple rules should involve more than just developing anonymous procedures for church and ecumenical instruments divorced from the people wherever they live — even if such procedures are just and participatory. If the rules are to fulfill their protective function, they would have above all to encourage and support sharing in and between local congregations and Christians. All initiatives and programmes aimed at strengthening and sharing community in the life of local congregations and churches should receive priority. This gives rise to a further rule: all initiatives and programmes which divide or create barriers in a congregation or church are contrary to the spirit of a sharing community.

One further consequence should be mentioned: sharing as meeting between people, as the exchange of experiences and spiritual testimonies has priority over the sharing of material resources. Indeed the sharing of resources follows upon the meeting between people. It is an expression of fellowship and a means of strengthening it. One of the most important lessons of ecumenical learning and renewal processes in the Northern churches is that these have been initiated by people who have been refreshed by the witness of Christians in other churches through the ecumenical encounter. One goal of the common commitment should be to reinforce these basic experiences of sharing.

4. It is vitally important that our commitment should not extend only to sharing in and between Christian churches and communities. Important as it is to pursue our priority goal of strengthening the exchange between local congregations as communities of sharing, it is at the same time true that a Christian congregation can only become a parable of shared life to the extent that it shares the goodness of God's creation with all human beings. In the course of the discussion in recent years there have been many stormy disputes as to whether sharing proves itself principally in fellowship and solidarity between Christians and churches or in solidarity with the poor in the struggle for justice and human dignity. The common commitment will have to deal concretely with these two dimensions of solidarity and to face — if not overcome — the element of tension in their relationship.

5. If the common commitment is understood as a framework of rules intended to clear the way for the realization of a sharing community in

and between the churches, then they must confine themselves to setting boundary marks. This makes it all the more important that they should be completed by examples and models of sharing community in a variety of contexts. Examples and testimonies of this kind drawn from the life of the churches at the present time are more important than appeals and recommendations, however urgent. They are in keeping with the spirit of sharing, for they encourage, challenge and stimulate us to move forward on the path of renewal. This will be the test of ecumenical solidarity in the years ahead.

One People

Affirmation on peace and justice

People
I believe in God, who is love and who has given the earth to all people.
I believe in Jesus Christ, who came to heal us, and to free us from all
forms of oppression.
I believe in the Spirit of God, who works in and through all who are
turned towards the truth.
I believe in the community of faith, which is called to be at the service of
all people.
I believe in God's promise to finally destroy the power of sin in us all, and
to establish the kingdom of justice and peace for all humankind.

Group A
I do not believe in the right of the strongest, nor the force of arms, nor the
power of oppression.

Group B
I believe in human rights, in the solidarity of all people, in the power of
non-violence.

Group A
I do not believe in racism, in the power that comes from wealth and
privilege, or in any established order that enslaves.

Group B
I believe that all men and women are equally human, and that God intends
for the world an order based on justice and love

Group A
I do not believe that war and hunger are inevitable and peace unattainable.

Group B
I believe in the beauty of simplicity, in love with open hands, in peace on earth.

People
I do not believe that suffering need be in vain, that death is the end, that the disfigurement of our world is what God intended. But I dare to believe, always and in spite of everything, in God's power to transform and transfigure, fulfilling the promise of a new heaven and a new earth where justice and peace will flourish.

Guidelines for Sharing

I

Out of abundant and outgoing love, God has created the world, and has given it to all humanity for faithful use and sharing. As recipients of God's gift of life, we are called to see the world through God's eyes, offering it in blessing through our own acts of love, sharing and appropriate use.

But, because of our sin and selfishness, we have misused God's gift. We have allowed the interests of a few to diminish the life of many. It has led to the rise of unjust structures which perpetuate dependence and poverty for the majority of the world's people. This surely is contrary to the purpose of God.

It is in the midst of this sinful reality that in Jesus Christ God offered God's very self for the life of the world. Jesus' self-emptying love on the cross leads us to repentance. It becomes the power and pattern of our sharing.

The presence of the Risen Lord in the power of the Holy Spirit enables us to break down barriers and renew structures, preparing for the coming of God's kingdom of justice and peace.

The new life given by the Holy Spirit in Christ creates us as a new people — members of one body, bearing one another's burdens and sharing together in God's gift of life for all.

In the eucharist, we offer to God ourselves and the whole of creation in its brokenness, and receive all things back anew. The eucharist sends us back into the world to be Christ's body, broken and shared for the life of the world.

As the first-fruits of the new humanity, the church is called to stand in solidarity with all people, particularly with the poor and the oppressed, and to challenge the value systems of this world.

Having confidence in the grace of God in Jesus Christ, who alone through the Holy Spirit enables us to live in obedience to the divine will, we, the participants in the world consultation on resource-sharing, coming from different regions, commit ourselves to a common discipline of sharing among all God's people.

II

In all such sharing we commit ourselves:

1. To a fundamentally new value system based on justice, peace and the integrity of creation. It will be a system that recognizes the rich resources of human communities, their cultural and spiritual contributions and the wealth of nature. It will be radically different from the value system on which the present economic and political orders are based and which lies behind the current crises like those of nuclear threat and industrial pollution.

2. To a new understanding of sharing in which those who have been marginalized by reason of sex, age, economic and political condition, ethnic origin and disability, and those who are homeless, refugees, asylum-seekers and migrants take their place at the centre of all decisions and actions as equal partners.

This means, for example, that:
— churches, councils and networks will establish for this purpose ecumenical mechanisms both nationally and regionally;
— equitable representation will be provided for women and youth in decision-making structures.

3. To identify with the poor and oppressed and their organized movements in the struggle for justice and human dignity in church and society. This in turn will imply the refusal to participate, either as giver or receiver, in ways of sharing that undermine this struggle.

4. To bear witness to the mission of God by identifying, exposing and confronting at all levels the root causes, and the structures, of injustice which lead to the exploitation of the wealth and people of the third world and result in poverty and the destruction of creation. This entails working for a new economic and political order.

This would mean, for example, that the churches of the North and the South commit themselves to strengthen and participate in the various anti-nuclear movements and to bring pressure upon their governments to stop nuclear testing and the dumping of nuclear waste. It will also mean joining with the people in their struggle against transnational corporations, militarism and foreign intervention and occupation.

5. To enable people to organize themselves and realize their potential and power as individuals and communities, working towards the kind of self-reliance and self-determination which are an essential condition of interdependence.

6. To be open to one another as friends on the basis of common commitment, mutual trust, confession and forgiveness, keeping one another informed of all plans and programmes and submitting ourselves to mutual accountability and correction.

This implies, for example, the implementation of mutual accountability and participation in decision-making between the South and the North.

7. To represent to one another our needs and problems in relationships where there are no absolute donors, or absolute recipients, but all have needs to be met and gifts to give, and to work for the structural changes in the institutions of the North and the South which this calls for.

8. To promote through words and deeds the holistic mission of the church in obedience to God's liberating will. We are convinced that in responding only to certain parts of the mission we distort and disrupt mission as a whole.

9. To participate in the struggles of people for justice, and thereby overcome all barriers between different faiths and ideologies which today divide the human family.

This means, for example, churches in East and West making use of all opportunities to strengthen the process of detente and integrating the resources freed by this process for ecumenical sharing.

10. To resist international mechanisms (such as the International Monetary Fund/World Bank) which deprive the people of the South of their resources — transferring for example their hard-earned capital, which is more than the aid they receive, in payment of foreign debt, thereby putting them in a state of perpetual dependence — contributing instead to a fundamental and just redistribution of the wealth and resources of a country including the wealth of its churches.

11. To devise ways of shifting the power to set priorities and terms for the use of resources to those who are wrongfully denied both the resources and the power, such as movements for social justice.

This would imply that participation of the South in the decision-making must not only be on a consultative basis as it is practised today.

12. To facilitate and encourage mutual involvement among the churches and people in the South who have common concerns, for example through the sharing of human resources.

13. To promote and strengthen ecumenical sharing at all levels, national, regional and international.

III

Ecumenical sharing of resources will take place at all these three levels:
— local;
— national/regional;
— international/inter-regional.

Relations between bodies at the three levels of sharing should be characterized by flexibility, complementarity and mutual power-sharing.

All levels of implementation should recognize and work towards the goal of an equitable representation of 50% women and 20% youth in all decision-making structures over the next five years.

At the local level

The initiative to obtain resources from national and international agencies should, as far as possible, be taken by the local community.

In situations where local ecumenical groups and churches are not working together and where it prevents resource-sharing, the process should be facilitated through local community action, and every effort made to encourage ecumenical cooperation among groups and churches.

At national and regional levels

Where national or regional mechanisms for resource-sharing do not exist, the need to set them up must be seen as a matter of urgency. These mechanisms may consist of representatives of churches, ecumenical groups and those popular or people's movements which are involved in the struggle for justice, peace and full human development.

These bodies should constantly and critically examine their own composition and activities and the power structures inside and outside the church, in order to achieve a more just and equitable resource-sharing. They should invite and facilitate both dialogue and critical assessment through visiting teams from the churches or groups with whom they share resources, to enhance mutuality and the sharing of power. International agencies should take part in the activities of these bodies only when invited.

It is important to educate public opinion in all our countries regarding the structural causes of world economic disorder. This can be done in theological training centres, for example, with the help of witnesses from among partners in sharing.

The regional level is where methods for monitoring resource-sharing can be most effectively established.

At the international level

International ecumenical resource-sharing bodies must be based on equal representation of the partners involved. They should complement the national/regional and local decision-making bodies, for example through round table structures and through the sharing of all relevant information, including financial, of projects/programmes among the partners involved.

All Christian World Communions and ecumenical organizations are called on to take part in the ecumenical sharing of resources through the WCC and to adhere to the discipline emerging from this consultation.

The WCC is called to a better integration of existing units and sub-units of the Council and, as far as possible, to coordinate the channelling of its resources through existing networks.

It is recommended that the WCC set up a mechanism to follow up the implementation of the discipline emerging from this consultation.

IV

We will follow this discipline ourselves. We will try to create a climate in which it is understood and welcomed. We will challenge our churches, their peoples and their agencies to accept it.

We will urge acceptance of this discipline beyond the membership of the WCC.

We will refuse cooperation when this discipline is explicitly being rejected.

We will create opportunities to develop new ecumenical partnerships to enable churches of different traditions and contexts to enrich one another.

We will support one another in our commitment. We undertake to give an account to each other and so to God, of the ways in which we have turned our words into deeds, within a period of three years.

Recommendations on women and youth

As a result of the meetings of women and youth at the consultation the following recommendations and comments were approved in plenary:

Women

The women's group recognizes that there is a very strong connection between the plight of women and the patriarchal interpretation of the Bible. Men's theology perpetuates a system where women are considered "less than". The theological section of the report must address this issue.

In the sharing of resources, women can offer new theological perspectives growing out of their experience (for example, "As Seen by Women" and "Asian Women Reading the Bible"). We strongly urge that during the Decade of the Churches in Solidarity with Women, the churches commit themselves to an in-depth study of and engagement with these perspectives.

1. We recommend that there must be 50% representation by women in all decision-making and consultative structures set up or changed as a result of this consultation, such as follow-up committees, local, national, regional, and international bodies and that all these bodies must reflect the liberating perspectives of women in their decisions.

2. We recommend that participants in this consultation commend to their organizations the Decade of the Churches in Solidarity with Women and encourage their support for it. In concrete terms, this means making available sufficient financial and other resources to initiatives which work towards justice for women and which enable their full participation in the societies in which they live.

3. We recommend that within the first five years of the Decade the goal be achieved of using 50% of the total annual flow of funds channelled through ecumenical bodies for programmes and activities empowering women, and their communities. These include:

a) those entirely planned and implemented by women;
b) those benefiting the larger community in which women play an equal part in decision-making and planning;
c) those which enable people to organize themselves and realize their potentials as individuals and communities.

Special emphasis should be placed on funding activities which:

a) enable women to develop in a systematic way visions and concepts for an alternative society based on justice, peace, equality, and an ecologically appropriate economy;

b) conscientize women of their rights and potential in their own societies;

c) provide leadership and skills training for women;

d) provide opportunity for regional meetings of women from all sectors and levels, particularly in the South-South context.

We urge decision-making bodies to scrutinize all funding requests to eliminate those which discriminate or work against the empowerment of women.

In 1992 there should be an evaluation by women of the achievements of this recommendation, both in financial and programmatic terms.

4. We also recommend that churches, church-related organizations and other donor agencies commit themselves to the 50% funding and decision-making patterns described above and submit themselves to the same review procedures. As these are likely to be bilateral relationships, it is important that the whole of God's family represented here, women and men, adopt and support this position as, in many cases, organizations are represented here by men alone.

5. We recommend that prior to the distribution of the audiovisual prepared for this consultation, alterations be made to the art work to make it inclusive of all God's family.

Youth

The youth group is not satisfied with the way young people have been invited to this consultation. The process has been going on for many years but youth have not been included. The primary concern of the youth group is the participation of young people in the ecumenical sharing of resources.

Young people around the world are bearing the heavy burden of the world's pain and injustice. Churches need to know and hear the experiences of young people.

Young people need solidarity, resources and support through the sharing of resources within the ecumenical movement.

Youth organizations, networks and projects need the support and the trust of those who themselves have once been young.

1. We recommend that in all decision-making bodies on resource-sharing there should be 20% youth including both women and men.

2. We recommend that 10% of all programme and project funds be designated for youth projects and programmes. These funds should include the administrative budgets of youth organizations.

One Earth

Leader
Let us affirm our desire that every woman and man and child be free to
walk and live in safety.

People
Yes, God of freedom and truth,
so say our hearts.

Leader
Let us affirm our desire to meet God in the world and in the meeting with
each other as God's daughters and sons.

People
Yes, God of grace and glory,
so say our hearts.

Leader
Let us affirm our desire to admire God's creation;
to nurture it, to protect it.

People
Yes, God of light and sun,
so say our hearts.

Leader
Let us affirm our desire to work for bread
for ourselves and all humanity.
To give and receive,
To share the bread of life.

People
Yes, God of life and death,
so say our hearts.

Leader
Let us affirm the surprising mystery and gift of each person and of life in a community of sharing.

People
Yes, God of hope and love,
so say our hearts.

A Common Discipline
of Ecumenical Sharing

The process

Eighteen working groups discussed the draft working document which had been prepared for the consultation. The document was divided into six sections:
— socio-political, economic and ecumenical context;
— biblical-theological convictions;
— local ecumenical sharing;
— national and regional ecumenical sharing;
— international ecumenical sharing;
— international ecumenical sharing: donor-recipient relationships.

Each of the sections was assigned to three working groups. Each group was asked to share experiences and discuss basic principles and new models. It was unavoidable that the groups would have to struggle with some overlap between the sections. The distinctions between local/ national, regional and international sharing were sometimes felt to be arbitrary. The following is drawn up from the written reports of the groups. The two parts on international ecumenical sharing have been merged into one, and the comments on models made by the groups put together.

SOCIO-POLITICAL, ECONOMIC AND ECUMENICAL CONTEXT

Ecumenical sharing of resources is not a process that can be confined to the churches. It takes place within a wider context of which it is a part, and which is characterized by political, socio-economic and cultural forces. Globally as well as locally, those forces result in imbalances and contradictions which leave the majority of the world's population marginalized and oppressed. There is a massive transfer of resources, including economic aid, but it is a well-known fact that the eventual beneficiaries are the rich, and that the poor continue to become poorer. Perhaps the most vivid illustration of how global injustice impinges on the poor is the international debt crisis. This analysis of the world economic system from the perspective of the poor has been made many times in ecumenical gatherings. For us it means that our efforts of ecumenical sharing must be in keeping with the struggle of the poor to realize a truly just global sharing of resources.

The churches participate in the unjust structures. As the WCC Central Committee said in its Message to the churches in 1980:

> Sadly, this disorder of the world too often has a mirror reflection in the churches, from the life of our congregations to the highest level of our institutions.

In the North as well as in the South our churches are part of the system which produces the rich and the poor, and some benefit from it while others suffer disadvantages. The churches are often tempted to seek their material and spiritual wellbeing within the prevailing economic and socio-political order. For this reason they hesitate to speak out and act against the forces that deprive many people in the third world, and increasingly also in the first, of their basic needs and rights. The churches are themselves centres of wealth and power which are not being used for the benefit of the whole human family. Even within the churches and the ecumenical movement there is no just sharing of resources. We recognize with sadness that our churches can be, and sometimes are, accomplices in injustice. On the other hand, there are also examples of churches which have taken the side of the poor, and we are encouraged by their witness.

The causes of injustice are not only economic but also cultural, theological and human. One aspect of this is the patriarchal/hierarchical influence on the structures of our societies and churches. It legitimizes the power of those who consider themselves to be of more value than others because of race, sex or age, particularly when they are white and male, and therefore think they have the right to dominate and exploit.

All international aid, including aid given by the churches, is part of the power structures that are responsible for many imbalances and injustices in the world today. Such aid is not neutral. It carries ideological components which reflect the value systems of the donors, i.e. the powerful. The trend towards privatization of the economy in the North in recent years is an illustration of this phenomenon. It impedes the community-oriented approach of sharing. Daily we can see examples of economic and cultural concepts of development which are imposed on the recipients of international aid. The good intentions and useful services of some agencies are necessarily limited by the system in which they are operating. On the whole, the international aid system is not able to change the trend of increasing poverty and marginalization. Economically speaking it often tends to perpetuate the unjust power structures. Churches and agencies for mission and development have been aware of the need for another quality of aid, but inevitably their assistance is also part of the system and marked by it.

There is a legitimacy of aid as Christian praxis. It is inherent to the gospel message and it cannot wait until justice will prevail. But we have to question the role of money and to ask ourselves how to deal with aid in such a way that it promotes justice and challenges the powers of oppression. It is not simply a matter of improving the aid system. Ecumenical sharing of resources must go beyond changes in the donor-recipient relationships of the churches to the issue of radical change in global and local structures. When this is the objective there can be an impact. Until now the churches have been mainly responding to the symptoms of the problems. There is need for more political advocacy and awareness-building in the affluent societies and conscientization of the victims of injustice around the world. The churches in the North as well as in the South must involve themselves in the struggle for justice. That means there are choices to be made and conflicts to be faced, also within their own fellowship, because sharing takes place mostly in conflict situations. For instance, in the South the churches have to examine their own complicity with regard to the domination of the North and their participation in unjust structures.

In the global context of a suffering world, the gospel also calls us to look beyond monetary sharing first on a more human, person-to-person level. The suffering peoples of the world are in need of solidarity. It is only after we begin to share our pains and burdens with one another that we are in a position to be able to understand what needs to be shared. The needs may not be monetary at all. The spiritual bankruptcy of the richer nations stands in need of the spirituality of the poorer nations. Peoples living under oppression in the Middle East, Southern Africa, and elsewhere around the world are crying out for a spiritual "being-with" in their suffering and an advocacy on their behalf. The ecumenical sharing of resources must be seen to encompass all types of resources in order to speak to our global context in a holistic way.

We as churches and WCC cannot dismantle the unjust world system but we must continue to raise the issues and at the same time look critically at our own aid operations. Over the past forty years or so the transfer of resources has become a major phenomenon in the life of the churches. Most of it is done via direct or so-called bilateral relationships and a smaller part through ecumenical channels. There is much dissatisfaction with the present systems of sharing, e.g.:

— the problem of power and the unwillingness to give up power;
— in much of what is called "sharing", money dominates a North-South donor-recipient relationship;
— women and youth are excluded from the mechanisms of resource-sharing; they have little or no way of participating in decision-making unless they set up their own instruments, and their concerns are not integrated at all levels;
— the existing patterns of assistance impede the growth of self-reliance;
— structures for mission and development often operate separately from one another;
— the role of intermediaries which prevent linking of communities at the local level; there is a growing demand for establishing direct relationships.

Another important factor in the present context is the growing impact of agencies which emphasize the direct response to needs and put less stress on issues of justice and structures. They gain acceptance because their procedures and priorities are appealing to many who find the ecumenical or bilateral systems complicated and not always responsive to their needs. Agencies of this nature with a Christian background are often related to "evangelical" movements. In many regions they are seen to identify themselves with neo-conservative socio-political groups and to act as vehicles of the political ideology of the latter.

From the time of its formation the WCC has provided a structure for sharing, i.e. the interchurch aid system, meeting of people, sharing of experiences and many forms of spiritual resources. The present attempt to hammer out an ecumenical commitment for sharing comes at a time of dissatisfaction particularly with the practice of mutual sharing. Views on what is wrong and why differ. For some the ecumenical channels are remote, depersonalized and unattractive. For others there is a lack of efficiency, professional competence and coordination between the different instruments of the WCC. It is estimated that less than 10% of the total flow of funds for interchurch aid, world service and development flows through the WCC. As for world mission, the mission agencies have no history of working with the ecumenical system, although some of them support regional and national ecumenical bodies through their partner churches.

Although the WCC has little direct impact on the major part of the flow of resources for mission and development, much of it is influenced by the spirit of the ecumenical movement. The WCC has an important role in providing the theological undergirdings from which the practices of ecumenical sharing evolve. The intention is not to channel more funds through the administration of the WCC but to make the guiding principles of ecumenical sharing more widely accepted by the churches. Some of the basic issues that lie at the heart of a common discipline of ecumenical sharing are:

— A radical change of minds away from the present money-oriented system to a new approach which is grounded in commitment.
— The commitment towards change of unjust structures as the objective of sharing, in order to eliminate injustice, poverty and oppression. This calls for identification, at every level of sharing, of the exploita- tive factors which need correction. It requires the readiness to under- stand aid as a process of reparation for the injustices inflicted on others.
— The willingness of the churches to take the side of the poor and the marginalized. Their voices should be listened to much more and they should be present in the decisions and actions of the churches.
— The self-reliance of the poor and the marginalized as the goal of sharing and solidarity. There may be different methods of achieving self-reliance according to context and culture, but sharing should always aim at the empowerment and selfhood of the recipient commu- nity.
— The involvement of people, and especially of women and youth. People from the local churches and communities, from grassroot movements and marginalized groups should become much more part of the sharing process.
— The comprehensive understanding of "mission" and "development" as parts of the overall mission of the church. This implies the need to work out new mechanisms bringing the two together.
— The search for conditions and criteria for receiving aid to identify clear values which undergird relationships in sharing, including South-South relationships. This calls for critical self-examination in the South and in the North.

— The recognition of different regional and cultural values and approaches of sharing. New ways of decision-making should become possible, which are freed from the oppressive aspects of the dominating Western culture and its economic system. The sharing of common concerns between and within regions should be promoted.
— The need for education in all processes of sharing and solidarity, including fund raising.

The vision of a new community that embraces and inspires all our relationships, bilateral as well as ecumenical, must remain with us. The commitment we seek is not to any one system but to a continuous search for the realization of that vision in our churches and communities.

BIBLICAL/THEOLOGICAL CONVICTIONS

Our sharing derives always from God's gift and God's call to community in Christ which are for all. The church is called to be a community and to share in God's mission to all people. This provides the biblical-theological convictions for the common discipline of ecumenical sharing.

Call to koinonia

1. The model of sharing

The Bible speaks of sharing in many places and in many ways, for example the feeding of the multitudes (John 6:1-14), the early church (Acts 2:43-47), the collection for Jerusalem (2 Cor. 8 and 9), Elizabeth and Mary sharing their spiritual joy (Luke 1:39-56). In the Jubilee Year (Lev. 25) and in the vision of the new earth (Isa. 65:17-25) sharing is a manifestation of justice; its aim is to eliminate the causes of poverty and exploitation. The covenant (Lev. 26:9-13) and the body (1 Cor.12:12-26) are metaphors of the biblical concept of koinonia.

Perhaps the strongest biblical paradigm of sharing is the eucharist. In the sharing of the bread and the wine we celebrate the communion with him who died for us and was raised, so that we share in his life, through the Holy Spirit, and receive life abundantly. Through this shared communion with Christ we enter into communion with one another. This is what constitutes the Christian community, the koinonia. It belongs to the essence of the church to be a community of sharing.

Only when the eucharist is really celebrated as the body broken for the world will it create and sustain a fellowship in which life is shared with all people. The search for the real meaning of the eucharist and for eucharistic unity cannot be separated from the task of deepening the ecumenical community of sharing. Moreover, in the celebration we acknowledge that the resources of creation are intended as God's gift of grace, for all to receive and to share. This sharing goes beyond the communion of the churches to the oikoumene, the whole inhabited earth, so that all God's people may enjoy the abundance of the resources of creation. We are reminded that all resources belong to God: "The earth is the Lord's and the fullness thereof, the world and those who dwell therein" (Ps. 24:1).

Recognizing that all God's children are made in God's own image, which we see in Genesis 1:26 as a plural image, we acknowledge that "there is neither Jew nor Greek, slave nor free, male nor female", but that we "are all one in Christ" (Gal. 3:28). When that is not reflected in the images and languages of God used by theological systems they may give rise to patriarchal domination which readily exploits people because of sex, race or caste. A call to koinonia calls us to re-examine such theological understandings that eliminate women or other groups in the community from sharing the life of Christ in all its fullness in all aspects of church and community life.

2. Sharing life

In Jesus' ministry we find the example of what it means to share life. He came "to serve and to give his life as a ransom for many" (Mark 10:45). He shared in the afflictions of the weak, the suffering, and the oppressed of his day. Sharing life is giving ourselves in compassion for those who suffer today in our world and whom we meet on our road, as did the Good Samaritan. Sharing life in a world community is to hear the cries of those who are exploited and are denied life because of unjust international structures, to identify with their suffering and support them.

3. Wholeness

The resources of creation are spiritual, human, cultural, as well as material. These dimensions of life should not be separated, as is often the case in the modern culture of many societies which cultivate the material values. The gospel underscores the unity between the spiritual and the material and leaves no place for the false dichotomy between the two. The material is a means to achieve sharing of life, as for example in the story of the Good Samaritan. In 2 Corinthians 8 the collection of the churches in Asia Minor for the church in Jerusalem is described as a fruit of their love and "abundance of joy". In our churches the disproportionate importance attached to the material over the spiritual and human has often degraded the wholeness of sharing. The ecumenical sharing of resources cannot function with a division between the spiritual and the material.

Call to mutuality...

1. ...in power sharing

In the relationships between individuals, groups, organizations and nations we have to assess whether the power that displays itself is a power that will liberate or oppress, heal or wound, love or hate. God's power is shown in love and justice: the self-emptying love of Christ (kenosis), who affirms the real power which the poor and oppressed can exert when they find the truth of God's good news. Jesus teaches us that love is the strongest power. He has shown us a way in which strength is revealed in surrender that does not become submission, and promised us the power of the Spirit to love and to serve. Empowerment is a process of enabling all God's people to bring their sharing together, affirming the dignity and capability of individuals and communities to be themselves. For us, that implies helping oppressed groups to expose unjust use of power and oppose it, and enabling them to exercise the power they have in themselves. It also means that we must listen to the poor and the marginalized and allow their voices to penetrate and change all our institutions. These are the victims of economic and racial oppression, but also the unemployed, people with disabilities, youth, women, the homeless, migrants, etc. They should have the power to take their own decisions in situations affecting their life and future. This empowerment is needed in both South and North.

2. ...in repentance

In all our reflections on sharing we must confess that we are living out of harmony with the demands of the gospel and are lacking concern for one another. Sin is a reality, individually and at the level of our institutions. Our sharing does not reflect the biblical teaching that it should arise from a compassionate concern for justice. As persons and as institutions we often seek influence over others through our gifts. We are tempted to attach more importance to money than to spiritual values. The marginalized and the powerless in our communities are often excluded from the centres of decision-making. In all our churches, agencies and ecumenical organizations there is always some competition for power and control. The sin of falling short of sharing is never on one side only, it is everywhere. Again and again we must be willing to admit our faults, forgive one another and make a new beginning. We are enabled to do so if we live by grace and have the mind of Christ who "though he was rich, yet for your sake became poor" (2 Cor. 8:9, also Phil. 2:5-8).

3. ...in participation

The church is a community. Ecumenical sharing of resources means that all members must be given a full part in the local communities and groups as well as in our institutions and decision-making bodies. Groups within the community like women, youth, people with disabilities, aged, unemployed are often marginalized. Yet their perspectives, resources and experiences are essential for the renewal of relationships and initiatives of empowerment and sharing. Their challenge and perception are necessary for our understanding of solidarity and justice. We must constantly seek patterns of decision-making which make it possible for all to take part. Perhaps our greatest difficulty has to do with the participation of the poor who are often the first to be excluded from our deliberations and decisions. We should not take decisions which affect an identifiable group of people without their participation.

4. ...in relationships

As churches and Christians we are both dependent on and responsible to each other because we have a common relationship with Christ as Lord. We are part of the universal church irrespective of our material wealth and our capacity to give money. Together we form a fellowship that is likened to the body: if one member suffers the others suffer too; if one rejoices, so do all.

God has entrusted to all many varied talents and gifts. No one can claim exclusive ownership of resources. We do not share what is ours; rather, we distribute and partake in what is God's. We all have needs, and we are called to accept each other in gratitude as givers and receivers. Our capacity for sharing is reflected in mutual relations of equality and selfhood.

5. ...in accountability

As churches, agencies and groups we have different perceptions of each others' identity, priorities, needs and resources partly because our own local situations differ greatly, and partly because our commitments may not be the same. We must listen to one another and help each other by interpreting situations and needs. Real openness and candour are essential. Accountability cannot only be reduced to responsible stewardship of the use of resources but demands mutual openness to questions about priorities, use of power, relationships and theological convictions. This spiritual responsibility for one another is also pertinent within local groups and agencies. We are accountable to one another, to the poor and ultimately to God. Maybe the most important question we must ask each other again and again is whether our deepest commitment is to those whom Jesus called the least of his people.

6. ...in structures

Our institutions and organizations reflect certain functional divisions which are necessary for the church to carry out its mission. But whenever structures perpetuate the tendency to separate the material sharing from the spiritual, or service and development from mission and evangelism, or political action from mission and development, whenever structures deny power to the poor and oppressed, or the commitment to justice, or the importance of non-institutional action groups, then those structures must be dismantled or transformed, and new ones built in their place.

The need for structural changes must not be allowed to be inhibited by problems caused by the size of our institutions and organizations, by the tendency towards centralization and by elitist attitudes.

Call to responsibility in the world

1. Sharing in the one mission of God

The fellowship of sharing is a means whereby the church seeks to live out its universality and fulfill its task of bringing God's love and justice revealed in Jesus Christ to all people. The focus of the church's proclamation and action is to restore the intended relationship between God, humanity and the creation. From this perspective there is no reason to separate mission from service and development. Our concepts of development may differ depending on cultural and social values. We may also have different views on what the mission of the church is. But all the activities of the Christian community in evangelism, diakonia, the struggle for human dignity, healing, peace and justice belong together in the one mission of God.

2. Sharing with all people

Christian sharing takes place in the midst of the life of people, in local situations of need and struggle. We must listen to and learn from the poor, the oppressed, the marginalized; share in their suffering and hope and confront those institutions, such as apartheid, which cause such suffering and injustice. We must take seriously the realities of people in their immediate communities and the opportunities for learning and sharing there. Taking part in the struggle of others begins in the local community and from there extends to people who live in other parts of the world. A church or group which wants to be in solidarity with others but is not involved in its own situation should learn to understand the link that exists between the issues of poverty and injustice at the global level and the situation at home. A partner who comes from outside should engage with the local community. These are essential prerequisites for sharing with people in distant places.

All over the world the sharing of resources involves far more than the Christian churches and agencies for mission and development. The majority of the poor are not in the Christian churches. Christians are working together with people of other faiths and convictions in the struggle for justice and peace. In some countries the church is a minority in the midst of a religiously plural environment. Elsewhere it is called to live out its faith in the context of a society that is strongly marked ideologically. Sharing life across religious and ideological barriers is part of our Christian obedience to the calling to be in solidarity with the poor and the oppressed and, indeed, with the whole human family.

LOCAL ECUMENICAL SHARING

Our local situations differ greatly. Ecumenical sharing does not mean the same for a congregation in a residential area in California, a church in rural South India or an Orthodox parish in Bulgaria. But for all three the ideal of a sharing church is found in the description of the first Christian community in Acts 2. For all of us, commitment to sharing and justice begins at home. A personal commitment is needed, reaffirmed and strengthened by those surrounding us in our local church, in our village or sector of town. Our awareness of each other's needs and gifts should be increased through a learning process, in which we may discover the vast human and spiritual resources of our communities. Some guidelines for sharing life with our neighbours are:
— to affirm actions that enhance the sharing of life, such as openness to learning from each other; taking part in each other's culture; being in solidarity with each other;

— to affirm the rights and power of our brothers and sisters;
— to affirm the inclusion of our neighbours in decision-making as we share life together;
— to affirm the enhancement of our neighbour's self-reliance;
— to affirm an attitude of living with openness and honesty with our neighbours in mutual responsibility;
— to ensure that in all that we do, every initiative is in accordance with God's mission to the whole world.

To share life means to engage each other; to share our humanness, our personhood, our culture, our love and compassion for each other; to be in community with each other locally (at home), nationally and globally.

This sharing of life with all our neighbours nearby and far off is impeded by socio-political and economic structures which tend to dismiss values that have no financial weight. For example much of the work done by women is not counted for economically, such as the role rural women in the South play in agriculture. Another example is the impact of modern technology which contributes more to the dislocation and exploitation of human communities and their environment than to their development, especially in the South. We as churches should strongly support alternative economic models that value the work of women and enhance the quality of life. The churches in the North should engage in strategies confronting the political and economic forces based in their own countries, such as transnational corporations, which exploit the people in the South. Changing of the structures which cause oppression and injustice must begin at the local level. The local churches should develop models of action and take steps to make themselves meaningful and effective instruments of change in their own situation.

Some of the ways and means to develop ecumenical sharing locally are:
1. To build up the life of the local church in the local community. In some places the priority will be to develop self-reliance through the use of local resources and to deepen the unity of the community; elsewhere to strengthen involvement of all irrespective of age, gender, social status; sharing in decision-making is an essential element for the life of the local community.

In many communities there still exist traditional patterns of sharing which have a great value and are in line with the biblical teaching. Every aid from outside the community should be checked for not disturbing these traditional patterns.

2. To involve the local church in the struggle of the poor and the marginalized in both South and North:

a) to learn from people's organizations such as women's and youth's organizations, workers' unions, base communities, etc. and to take part in actions aiming at empowering the poor, women and youth and bringing justice to the local situation;

b) to learn from marginalized and oppressed groups in the community and to take part in their struggle against injustice; these could be migrant workers in some countries, elsewhere indigenous people or the oppressed majority as in South Africa.

3. To share more across denominational barriers — in worship, study and action — and to struggle for the unity of the church in the local situation.

4. To share across cultural, racial and socio-economic barriers — pairing congregations and groups from different backgrounds within the community, addressing together the issues which divide and unite them.

5. To participate in solidarity actions, vigils, prayers, etc. on behalf of people in other parts of the world, linking the life of the local congregation or group to the global community.

These international solidarity actions will have credibility only when they are not an escape from involvement in actions against local forms of oppression and injustice.

6. To educate for sharing, solidarity and justice, using the examples of the local situation. In some places the emphasis may be on the sharing of spiritual resources; in others, on contributing to projects. But the principle remains — all churches should learn to think and act ecumenically; all should learn to be givers and all should learn to be receivers.

7. To organize programmes of exchange and visits to build up solidarity among people and new relationships among communities, e.g. within the South, from the South to the North and vice versa, within the North, with socialist countries:

a) bringing people from outside into the life of the local congregation or group, helping them to learn and learning from them;

b) enlisting members of the congregation or group in visits in other parts of the world and in seminars, work-camps, short-term service, etc.

Such visits and exchanges can be meaningful signs of "sharing without money". They can stimulate and facilitate local sharing. For example, visitors from other parts of the world who are victims of exploitation can point to the same kind of victimization in the place they visit, or to the links with their own situation. They can share their experience of suffering, their Christian witness and their sense of community and solidarity.

NATIONAL AND REGIONAL ECUMENICAL SHARING

The socio-political, economic and cultural situations of our nations and regions differ widely. There is much divergence also in the tradition, history and life of our churches, church-related groups, social action movements and in the ecumenical movement. Ecumenical sharing is a process of cooperation and unity providing a fellowship, nationally and regionally, in spite of these divergences. The ultimate expression of sharing is in our suffering together in the body of Christ. Within our nations and regions we as churches should share in the sufferings of the other members of the body and of the human family. We must involve ourselves in issues of justice, of peace and of solidarity with the poor and the marginalized, in order to transform the unjust political and economic structures.

Sharing of resources, whether bilateral or multilateral, means the transformation of structures where they are unjust. As partners we must be committed on three levels:

1. *Human and spiritual:* We must learn to know each other better in our sufferings, our struggles, our hopes and achievements.

2. *Material and financial:* The funds transferred from the churches and agencies in the North to their partners in the South cannot wipe out the plundering of the countries of the third world. This material and financial sharing must therefore aim at a genuine redistribution of the world's resources, for example through the application of land rights and other means bringing justice to the deprived.

3. *Political and economic:* As men and women in our churches in the South and the North committed to the liberation of all people we are taking part in the pursuit of a political order which is different from that of today's world. This order must take shape through our participation in each other's daily struggles.

Some principles of a discipline of sharing that seeks to promote justice are:

— A spirit of repentance in the church for its involvement in the political and economic exploitation of the poor.

— The readiness of the church to divest itself of its own institutional power and prestige, and to use its power responsibly for the good of

the poor. When the church accepts to suffer with people who struggle for their human dignity it will experience that in losing its life it will find life.
— An intentional effort to bridge the gap between the churches and the poor. This means more than being engaged in advocacy for the poor. The churches must be part of their struggle, suffer with them and humbly participate in their liberation.
— Genuine power-sharing as the mark of relations between communities. For instance those who transfer funds may not in any way lay claim on the project put into effect by the group for whom the transfer is intended.
— A vigorous concern for minorities and groups in the church and in society whose rights are not recognized, e.g. women.
— Readiness to join with people of other faiths and of secular ideologies in the struggle against injustice and oppression, thus expressing the goal of "shalom" which God intends for the whole human family.
— A joint effort of the churches in the South and the North to inform and educate each other, so that we all may be better equipped to put into practice our vision of sharing.

There are many situations where the churches must stand in solidarity with the oppressed and the victims; for example:
— *South Africa*, by bringing pressure upon the government and upon multinational corporations in their country to end their support of the apartheid regime.
— *Middle East*, by working with those who seek a just political solution and influencing the governments to help bringing peace to the region.

Among the means to achieve ecumenical sharing nationally and regionally are:
1. To undertake mutual assessment and evaluation through team visits, either within a country or between countries in the same region.
2. To set up new structures for cooperation and better use of resources ensuring mutual representation and adequate coordination of all partners.
3. To promote the participation of women and youth by achieving within an agreed-upon period of time the goal of 50% women and 20% youth in all decision-making bodies.
4. To encourage mutual sharing between Christian communities across national boundaries of neighbouring nations, in order to dispel misunderstanding and misconceptions of the neighbour.

5. To develop a more effective system of sharing of information and documentation between churches in different nations, in order to counteract misinformation received through the public media and to provide a sound basis for analysis and joint action.

With special emphasis on the national level:
The churches and groups and the national council should engage in a serious review of the existing patterns of sharing, with a view to:
a) examine the proportion of the resources for local, national and international action used denominationally and ecumenically;
b) analyze the power relations in the national situation.
They should establish means whereby they could together:
a) engage in a joint process of determining priorities for their mission and service;
b) establish full transparency about their bilateral and ecumenical relationships;
c) interpret the instruments and structures for international ecumenical sharing to and from the local churches and groups.

There should be closer cooperation between churches of differing traditions, especially in situations of long-standing isolation and even hostility between Christian communities in the same country. Respect and preservation of the gifts of different ethnic and cultural communities within the churches are necessary, in the context of the larger unity of the body of Christ.

Churches and groups in the same country should join their efforts of hospitality for the strangers within the gates: the homeless, the refugees, asylum-seekers, etc.

The churches in the rich countries have a particular responsibility to:
a) consider seriously the implications of their investments for the perpetuation of poverty and oppression;
b) struggle against the exploitation of the poor and of the resources of the South by their governments and corporations of the North.

Wherever the church is placed it must be ready to call on the national leaders to use their power responsibly on behalf of the poor. This responsibility is especially great in those countries where Christians form the majority of the population.

With special emphasis on the regional level:
The churches and networks in the region, together with the regional council should undertake a review of existing methods of sharing of resources and where necessary develop new ones, to:

a) strengthen sharing and solidarity within the region, especially the sharing of the vast human resources and experiences;
b) coordinate international ecumenical sharing at the regional level;
c) develop more sharing between regions.

They should consider the possibility of setting up regional centres for gathering and distributing information on the conditions in the countries of the region.

INTERNATIONAL ECUMENICAL SHARING

The problems we face in international ecumenical sharing are many and diverse. There is no one system or scheme that can offer all the solutions. What is needed therefore is a common discipline to guide the international sharing relationships of the churches. Such a discipline should apply to sharing through ecumenical as well as through bilateral channels. Almost all these instruments for international resource-sharing which exist today reflect a Western mindset. It is very important that careful consideration be given to the role of culture in drawing up the discipline so that cultures in other parts of the world can have an impact on the relationships and the instruments of cooperation. The substance of each relationship, whether there is an element of financial aid or not, should be spiritual sharing and solidarity. This means also sharing of insights into the gospel arising from cultural heritage, commitment to liberation and involvement in the struggle, and sharing in the suffering and pain of other members of the body of Christ. The discipline should embody mutual dependency, i.e. no giving without an expression of the need to receive from the other, and no receiving without the offer to share from one's own resources. The discipline must enhance the visibility of the many forms of non-material sharing which are going on but are often not recognized because they cannot be counted in dollars and cents.

Some principles of a common discipline of ecumenical sharing are:
— the understanding that resources are held in common;
— the understanding that resource-sharing must enable each church to fulfill its total mission, which includes proclamation, justice and service;
— a preferential option for the poor in all actions of sharing and integrity in the concern for the poor both in one's own society and abroad;
— the integration of international sharing of resources (both personnel and finance) with international approaches to issues of justice;

— special emphasis on people-to-people sharing as the most effective means to learn about one another, share in the suffering of others and build up solidarity;
— sharing of decision-making between the partners at all levels of the process by which decisions are taken;
— participation of 50% women and 20% youth (men and women) in all decision-making bodies on resource-sharing;
— commitment of the partners to share all the information they hold (with the understanding that security may have priority over information in some situations);
— openness ("transparency") and accountability in a process of mutual commitment through which covenant relationships may be built up; this includes the acceptance of "mutual distrust" recognizing that mutual correction and confrontation might be required;
— an intentional effort of agencies for mission and development to expose themselves and share their problems with the churches, councils and groups to whom they relate;
— the development of criteria for resource-sharing from the priorities of the local situation where the project is located;
— the development of regional systems of resource-sharing from within each region;
— priority to people-to-people sharing in and between the regions of the South; this means that structures in the South should be encouraged and enabled to develop criteria and projects, and that agencies should allocate undesignated resources for this priority;
— the readiness of all bilateral partnerships to face the challenge of also sharing ecumenically;
— the acceptance by each church, council, agency or group of its responsibility to make international sharing of resources work within the parameters of the common discipline.

In order to put into practice the discipline for international ecumenical sharing the following ways and means are suggested to all the partners:
1. To develop and resource concrete programmes of spiritual and human sharing, e.g. worship resources (use of Ecumenical Prayer Cycle), evangelism, theological insights, consciousness-raising and confidence-building.
2. To involve each church/group from time to time in ecumenical visitation programmes (hosting or sending or both).

3. To involve people from the "grassroots" in all forms of spiritual and human sharing (e.g. visits, solidarity actions, celebrations, etc.).

4. To use the so-called "partnerships" of dioceses/districts/local churches/groups as opportunities for ecumenical sharing and learning.

5. To increase exchanges such as within the South, within the North, between the South and Eastern Europe, from the South to the North, etc. using existing networks and building up new relationships.

6. To link churches, groups and movements in different parts of the world which are working on similar issues of justice, peace, empowerment of the poor and oppressed, in order to build up solidarity networks. Careful study to determine priorities and strategies for such networking should be undertaken.

7. To develop new, creative ways whereby churches in countries with government regulations which restrict their participation in international sharing can take part more fully.

8. To accept some basic principles of external assistance such as:
   a) The establishment of joint mechanisms in which the partners involved participate equally;
   b) no involvement of the external partner in a local situation without dialogue with the local churches and groups;
   c) setting of priorities in terms of the local situation;
   d) decentralized and shared decision-making on projects;
   e) multilateral evaluation of projects and relationships with the partners involved and the help of others.

9. To promote the participation and the concerns of women and youth by achieving within an agreed-upon period of time the goals of:
   a) 50% women and 20% youth in all consultative and decision-making meetings and structures on international sharing;
   b) 50% of funds for projects in which women have had an equal voice in decision-making and 10% of funds for youth projects.

10. To strengthen the ecumenical cooperation through existing instruments for ecumenical sharing and new ones to be created.

11. To build up a network of information on the totality of sharing, i.e. ecumenical as well as bilateral.

12. To increase the participation in existing loan schemes (e.g. Ecumenical Development Cooperative Society (EDCS) and Ecumenical Church Loan Fund (ECLOF) and to initiate new ones, as loans by their nature can serve as a model for resource-sharing.

With regard to churches, councils and groups when receiving external resources:

Churches, councils and networks of groups should establish ecumenical instruments nationally or locally in which representatives of marginalized groups would participate, with a view, among other things, to:
a) define priorities applicable to the country or region;
b) open up ecumenical sharing to partners who are not depending on ecumenical structures generally;
c) decide on projects for which external resources are requested (material and spiritual);
d) work out for the country or region conditions for accepting resources and revise these regularly;
e) share information about relationships and resources and establish transparency;
f) promote the use of loan schemes;
g) ensure the full participation of women and youth.

These local partners should establish joint mechanisms with external partners to:
a) discuss priorities;
b) share information;
c) agree on external resourcing of projects.

This could be achieved by inviting representatives of external partners to certain meetings of the national ecumenical instruments (as mentioned above).

The local partners should agree not to bypass the ecumenical instruments and to apply the priorities and conditions for acceptance of resources also to their direct, bilateral relationships with external partners.

They should be ready to listen to and learn from the opinions and critical evaluations of others in similar situations who have gained experience in involvement with the poor and the marginalized.

Local churches and groups should facilitate the conscientizing of external partners by providing opportunities for dialogue and education.

With regard to churches and support agencies when sharing resources:

Churches and their agencies for mission and development should engage in an ongoing review process and theological reflection of how resources are shared, with the help of churches/groups from other parts of the world:

— to formulate their policy in the light of the priorities and the conditions for acceptance of resources by those with whom they share; and
— to evaluate relationships and structures for world mission, service and justice issues.

As part of this process, they should seek ecumenical consultation prior to decisions on specific policy issues and on new actions which are being considered. They should not build up structures outside their country when organized networks already exist or when the local churches or groups may be in a position to establish these.

The churches and their agencies for mission and development should set up programmes of advocacy for the poor and involve themselves in concrete actions on behalf of those to whom financial assistance is directed, with their guidance and participation. They could undertake activities in the economic field, e.g. related to the prices of agricultural products from small farmers or to the foreign debt problem. Through action-based education programmes for mission and development they should inform their supporters of the unjust and oppressive conditions that make financial aid a necessity. Such programmes should be initiated where they do not yet exist and more resources must be made available for education.

Besides their international commitment these churches and their agencies must also engage in actions with the powerless in their own country, e.g. groups which are marginalized for reasons of sex or age, economic and social situation, ethnic or racial origin, religion, etc.

The churches and their agencies should use an increasing portion of all their resources to enable forms of spiritual and human sharing and solidarity actions, and set aside part of these resources for South-South sharing. They should set a goal for increased sharing through ecumenical instruments (undesignated or block allocation) and a timeline for reaching the goal through incremental stages.

The churches and agencies should invite and facilitate both dialogue and critical assessment by visiting teams from the churches/groups with whom they share resources, to enhance mutuality and transfer of power.

With regard to the World Council of Churches:

The WCC should improve its internal sharing of resources among the various sub-units and their networks. It should encourage action programmes of networks of solidarity, forms of spiritual sharing, partnerships, etc. to help the churches, agencies and groups overcome some of the shortcomings of the project system. It should facilitate team visits and develop ways of reporting widely on these events to the constituency.

The WCC should work towards the goal of undesignated funding of its instruments of ecumenical sharing through specific agreements with the churches and agencies. It should facilitate the functioning of the joint mechanisms and of ongoing consultation between the partners involved in international ecumenical sharing.

The round table structure should be further developed and deepened as a valid concept for multilateral cooperation and solidarity, in order to:

a) experiment with power-sharing;
b) broaden the participation of the poor, the marginalized, women, youth, etc.;
c) promote block grant funding;
d) include mission agencies;
e) integrate the spiritual and financial aspects of sharing;
f) involve the different WCC sub-units concerned;
g) include as many member churches and groups in the country concerned as possible.

These round tables should become instruments of solidarity for which money is no longer the main motivation. Similar structures should also be envisaged for countries in the North.

Other means by which the WCC could further the discipline of international ecumenical sharing include the development of a data bank of information, a thorough analysis of income-generating projects, an accounting system that would be acceptable for all and the development of a set of criteria for the ecumenical cooperation of support agencies (this proposal, called accreditation system, was made by the world consultation on Inter-Church Aid, Refugee and World Service, Larnaca, November 1986).

The WCC should provide opportunities for the partners globally:

a) to evaluate international sharing (ecumenical and bilateral);
b) to facilitate the funding of ecumenical instruments of sharing;
c) to facilitate the funding of ecumenical structures (national, regional and global) and of South-South sharing.

MODELS

In spite of many good intentions, the system of providing external resources has often perpetuated and sometimes increased dependency. On the other hand, there are situations where development and popular movements take place without external aid. Self-reliance of the poor must be the aim of any sharing process. Symbolic new models of sharing alone will not reverse the trend of dependency. What we need are steps that will change the existing system. Some guiding principles in this search for models are:

— The goal of self-reliance. Some external aid aims at making the church structures self-reliant in the hope that the community at large will follow. New models may be sought in the role of the church as an instrument enabling the community through its self-governing structures to use its own potentials to gain self-reliance.
— The decentralization of mechanisms for decision-making. Some decentralized models are proposed in the report of the Asia preparatory consultation (Singapore, 29-31 March 1987).
— Joint decision-making by local and external partners. Regional, sub-regional and national forums should bring together churches, councils, grassroot organizations, mission and development agencies to decide on priorities.
— The inclusion of bilateral relationships in joint structures at the different levels. Bilateral and ecumenical models should inform, enrich and correct each other.
— The increase of undesignated funding and of the use of block grants.
— The equal participation (i.e. 50%) of representatives of local or grassroot communities in bodies where decisions on funding are taken.
— The extension of the concept of round table structures to countries in the North. Models of sharing of this type could promote new understandings of interdependency and solidarity.

One Bread

Leader

Sisters and brothers in Christ, we are gathered here this morning to celebrate the eucharist. In many ways, this may well be the central event of this conference for, from the very beginning, resource-sharing discussions have held up the eucharist as the most appropriate biblical paradigm on sharing. It has been said that "ecumenical sharing is the mark of a community rooted in the eucharist which confesses Jesus Christ as the life of the world".

The bread and wine which are brought to the altar symbolize that the whole of creation belongs to God. And yet, these very material symbols become to us, at this eucharist, that which nourish our spiritual life, reminding us that there is no dichotomy between the "material" and the "spiritual" in sharing life. The one bread which we would break is an affirmation that the creation is given by God, redeemed through Christ and sustained by the Spirit.

The eucharist is the supreme symbol of sharing also because here we celebrate God's self-giving, God's own sharing of life with and for the world. We who participate in this sharing cannot but become part of a community that has this spirit of sharing as the centre of its life.

But before we approach this mystery which Christ has prepared for us, let us confess our sins, recalling the ways in which we fave failed to live out our calling.

Confession

People
Most merciful God,
We confess that we are in bondage to sin and cannot free ourselves.

We have often sought to own this world, our life and all we possess,
not remembering that they belong to you;
We have not loved you with our whole heart.
We have often been unmindful of the needs of others,
unconcerned of their cries;
We have not loved our neighbours as ourselves.
We have sinned against you by what we have done,
and by what we have left undone.
For the sake of your son Jesus Christ, have mercy on us.
Forgive us, renew us and lead us,
so that we may delight in your will and walk in your ways,
to the glory of your holy name. Amen.

Leader
May the Almighty God who gave Jesus Christ to die for us,
forgive us our sins and bring us to life eternal. Amen.

The major presentations were given by
Sithembiso Nyoni from Zimbabwe and
◄ Konrad Raiser from the Federal Republic
1 of Germany

2 ▲

▼ 3

(3) Pablo Sosa from
Argentina and (4)
Patrick Matsikenyiri from
Zimbabwe shared their
gifts of music and
singing in the worship
services

(5) Christopher
Duraisingh from India
led the Bible studies

▼ 5

4 ▼

6 ◀

7 ▼

8 ◀

(6) Delegates — relaxed but full of attention

(7) Bishop Nifon, member of the planning group, and Huibert van Beek, secretary for ecumenical sharing of resources at the WCC and organizer of the conference, at the opening session

(8) Bishop Uwadi from Nigeria speaking during plenary

(9) Women played a key role at El Escorial. From left to right, Brigalia Bam, Jeanne Moffat, Nimalka Fernando, Anne Kerepia, Nashilongo Elago and Nora Chase at the presentation by the women participants

9 ▼

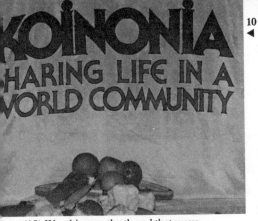

10 ◀

▶
11

(10) Worship was the thread that wove each day of the conference into the next

(11) Morning worship on the theme "One Light"

12 ◀

13 ▼

▲ 14

(12-15) The closing worship, on the theme of "koinonia", centred on an act of footwashing symbolizing commitment and the sharing of the bread as the sign of community. It ended in spontaneous joy and celebration

▶
15

(16) The schedule was heavy but there were also moments for relaxation

(17) Enjoying the autumn sun while reading group reports
(18) Meals brought together different people each day

(19) For those who were able to stay on an extra day: the excursion to the old city of Toledo
(20) A rehearsal of the choir which led singing during worship

Regional Group Discussions

Regional perspectives on the issues of ecumenical sharing were discussed in eight regional groups. These regional meetings took on particular importance as they became the main forum for discussing the draft of the proposed discipline (i.e. the Guidelines). Representatives of the regions of the South came together for one inter-regional meeting. The findings of the regional meetings are summarized hereafter. As the regional groups adopted their own process of working and reporting these records vary in style and length.

Africa

The group first discussed the participation of the African participants and their input into the consultation. It was agreed that the ideas developed by the group should be clearly stated in the working group meetings and the plenaries. In order to facilitate this process a small group was set up to summarize the discussions and the report of the Africa pre-consultation in one single paper.

The following points were noted in relation to resource-sharing.

Africa has been sharing its resources since time immemorial. It has often been forced to do so: human resources (slave trade, forced/migrant/cheap labour) and natural resources (minerals, crops, etc.). To the Africans, the flow of funds from the North is seen as the return of some crumbs of what was taken away over centuries.

The Western countries have extracted the wealth of Africa and continue doing so in the form of interest on billions of so-called foreign debt. These debts originated with the creation of the IMF and the World Bank which were designed to make the third world forever indebted to the West. While African currencies are considered worthless, African raw materials are highly valued.

There is much sharing of resources and of suffering in Southern Africa. The struggle in Angola, Mozambique and Zimbabwe would not have succeeded without the sharing of suffering by the people in the surrounding countries. Those who flee South Africa, Mozambique and Angola because of the oppression and destabilization of the apartheid regime are received, fed and housed by the people across the borders who share their homes and resources without counting the cost. Sometimes, this sharing is costly to their very lives.

All resources belong to God and are received freely from God. Those who give should therefore give freely. Human beings have been given responsibility and depend on God's forgiveness. They cannot form a forgiving community if they do not give the resources they hold to those in need, without strings attached. Sharing of financial resources must be done in a just way, recognizing that none is a perpetual giver and none a perpetual receiver.

Models of sharing of resources should be just and not based on sharing done out of surplus or excess sympathy which makes a perpetual beggar of the receiver. The dependency syndrome and beggar mentality have developed out of a distorted concept of sharing of resources by our ecumenical partners.

Sharing of resources should therefore include the sharing of power and decision-making which creates interdependency between the partners instead of making the other perpetually dependent. This is empowerment as mediated in the New Testament, enabling people to use their capacities and to become the people of God as God would like us to be.

Africans can share their rich spiritual traditions with the Western partners whose life-style has made them spiritually barren. There should be no strings attached to the sharing of cultural and spiritual resources. But the African participants in the consultation should not overstate their spiritual contribution. They should emphasize the vital importance of the economic and political issues for Africa.

The group spent some time on self-examination and criticism. One of the issues raised was that of the efforts made to maintain the expensive structures inherited from the missionary societies. Another area where Africans should liberate themselves was the sharing of the gospel and theological perspectives, and of their traditional religious and cultural values. The urgent need for sharing of information among Africans was underlined. There is no effective sharing in Africa. The North seems to be better informed about African political and economic issues than the Africans themselves.

Asia

The first meeting was an attempt to introduce ourselves, as well as to look into the objectives of the consultation, taking the Asian perspectives into account.

A number of concerns were identified, i.e. what constitutes an ecumenical discipline, learning past lessons vis-à-vis the project system, need to inform and get mandate from official levels, and a code of conduct in simple, firm and jargon-free language.

The discussions could be summed up under the headings: (1) context of resource-sharing; (2) mechanisms.

The context of resource-sharing is wider than the churches, taking into account the political, socio-economic and cultural conditions in which sharing is done.

Sharing is defined as involvement in the struggles for justice in conflict situations, where the poor need to empower themselves not only in terms of transfer and sharing in decision-making but with the goal of overcoming the roots of poverty and powerlessness.

Participation of the poor as active partner is imperative in all areas for the sharing of resources.

Churches and action groups are both invited to participate in the act of sharing human, material and non-material resources in the spirit of love and complementarity. In a number of situations where the people are actively engaged in struggles for justice and peace, solidarity support outside the formal church structures is necessary to widen the base of the poor in struggle.

The commitment to a discipline of sharing is an attempt to make sharing an experience of life in community. When we involve ourselves in sharing of resources, are we "in business" or are we in community?

There is a need to share non-material resources that could also underscore self-reliance in non-quantitative terms.

Sharing is broader than the structures of the churches.

Both the giver and the receiver have to say what they have to offer to each other.

Resource sharing should reflect and arise out of an ongoing relationship that sustains mutual responsibility and accountability.

What mechanisms do we see as appropriate? There are a number of ways to make sharing of resources ecumenical and multilateral: joint ways of setting priorities, transparency, mutual accountability, and better coordination of the mechanisms of giving.

Solidarity support should be extended to groups outside present ecumenical structures of churches and action groups.

There is a danger of centralization of mechanisms of resource-sharing. What happens to churches and action groups that do not have access to resources?

The group then discussed the first draft of the statement presented in plenary and the following main points were raised.

What has been presented in the introduction is a generous God, but we suggest that we present a self-emptying incarnate God who suffers with people who are victims of the unjust structures. It is necessary to confess the present dominance and dependence among societies and peoples.

We propose a discipleship of sharing in place of discipline.

In all our sharing, we commit ourselves to:
— a new inclusive understanding of all those who are marginalized in our societies;
— a fundamentally new value system based on justice, peace and the integrity of creation;
— complete identification with the poor and oppressed in all their suffering and struggles, and in so doing, confront the root causes of poverty;
— realization of potentials for power as individuals and as communities of interdependence among equals;
— mutual accountability, mutual correction and trust;
— the need to be both givers and receivers and not to behave like donors without needs and receivers who do not share;
— working together across all barriers of faith and ideologies;
— contributing to the fundamental and just distribution of wealth and resources in our countries;
— shifting power and setting priorities and terms for those who are denied both power and resources.

We commit ourselves to follow this discipline and to create a climate of understanding among all the parties to the sharing process. We will continue to challenge the churches and agencies to be faithful to this discipline.

Caribbean
The group looked first at the message of the Caribbean pre-consultation and noted that it raised most of the relevant questions coming out of the

region. The pre-consultation had also indicated ways in which the Caribbean has been sharing with others, and not simply receiving. However, there was as yet no firm proposal as to the management of resource-sharing involving the WCC and the Caribbean.

Therefore the world consultation should propose concrete mechanisms to facilitate and improve ecumenical sharing of resources.

There should also be a mechanism to make it incumbent upon partners to account adequately for the way they have used resources made available to them. This is in keeping with the principle of good stewardship. In the area of accountability there is need for openness and for the establishment of criteria that are current and relevant in the culture of those who benefit from resource-sharing.

The use of bilateral channels for resource-sharing by some Caribbean churches is not wrong in itself but may weaken the role of the Caribbean Conference of Churches at a time when it is politically inadvisable to do so. The information on such bilateral sharing should be made available to the CCC and where necessary endorsement should be sought from the CCC.

The group made the following comments in relation to the first draft of the proposed discipline for sharing.

The specific concerns that are of crucial importance particularly for countries of the poorer South should not be overlooked. Otherwise the suggested guidelines would not hold out much possibility of moving the process of resource-sharing from where it is at the present time.

The theological rationale should be worked over. Some use could be made of the concepts and insights emerging from the Bible studies.

The proposed discipline for sharing should address the real issues of the world economic system and political order. Otherwise the consultation would be lacking in purpose. While the advice that the consultation should arrive at measures that are manageable and practicable is sound, resource-sharing could hardly be discussed without locating the resources available to the churches worldwide within the context of the resources available to the countries in which the churches are set. The question of economic disparity between the rich North and the poor South cannot be avoided.

The group suggested therefore that representatives from the regions of the South (Africa, Asia, Caribbean, Latin America, Middle East, Pacific) should get together to look at the draft of the proposed discipline and present a common line as to how it might be changed. (Representatives from the South met for this purpose but it was eventually agreed that each region would present its comments to the plenary.)

In a final discussion the group noted that most of its suggestions had been incorporated. Concerning the implementation the group felt that unless the relevant mechanisms are put into place, resource-sharing will proceed in much the same way as before the consultation. Each region should therefore appoint a monitoring team and in addition, there should also be a group composed of representatives from the regions to monitor the follow-up. The consultation should agree on the principle, while details could be worked out later. The WCC should be the facilitator of the monitoring process.

Europe

After having discussed the European context the group agreed on the following comments in relation to the proposed discipline for sharing.

With regard to decision-making: All those who will be affected by decisions must be included in the decision-making process.

With regard to a new value system: Human beings, human resources and relationships between people ("sharing life") are more important than material resources.

With regard to solidarity: To be in solidarity with the poor, the oppressed, migrants, asylum-seekers, ethnic minorities, the unemployed and all who are ignored, and to open ourselves up to their suffering.

With regard to the causes of injustice: To bear our witness by renouncing our global economic and political disorder, and by acting against all that creates or keeps alive the systems of injustice, poverty and destruction.

With regard to interdependence: To enable people to realize their potential and power as communities and as individuals, so that relationships of equality can grow.

With regard to mutual accountability: We must learn from new patterns of sharing like CEVAA and CWM to make sure that churches and organizations in the South are really in control of decisions which affect them.

With regard to the total task of the church: Churches, agencies and action groups must be seen as parts of God's one mission working in mutual trust.

With regard to barriers between faiths and ideologies: We cannot work with systems and beliefs which deny the right of the poor to justice and liberation or to the integrity of creation.

With regard to the redistribution of resources: A 5% share of the income of churches and organizations and the setting up of new solidarity funds in the North are called for, with a more just use of the lands and other wealth of the church worldwide.

The group accepted the calls coming from the women and youth groups.

Latin America

In seeking to define the region's criteria in relation to the working document and the guidelines presented for discussion, the group based their reflections on the regional pre-consultation held in April 1987 at Lima in Peru.

The group's reactions revolved around two central positions: the biblical and theological foundations for ESR, and the principles and criteria of sharing on the basis of the positive and negative experiences of the local and regional groups.

Biblical-theological bases

Giving and receiving are not just a question of money. Christian sharing is nourished on the following:

a) In everything he did Jesus Christ shared. His whole life was a sharing and even his death was a gift so that we can have life. Sharing is a whole-hearted act which mainly involves giving life and receiving it.

b) Receiving and giving are liberating acts. Those who receive can give something of themselves. No one is so poor that they cannot share something. Those who give from their superabundance are not practising the liberty of love.

c) The practice of service cannot be separated from the other aspects of mission. We are challenged to include proclamation, worship, fellowship in communion and service with witness and giving.

d) Sharing is essentially a community act. The eucharist as a basic symbol of sharing is not a private act. It is linked with spirituality in community.

e) Sharing is a daily practice which cannot be isolated from the daily struggle for life and against death. Sharing arises out of the experiences of the people. Crisis and hope, joys and sorrows, troubles and triumphs are shared.

Criteria and principles based on experience

Any new proposals about ESR must be based on regional, national and local realities and there must be no attempt to treat the contextual differences as unimportant. It follows that a group of people gathered together in a world consultation cannot take decisions for a whole region. It may be easier for agencies or organizations to attend such an event with ready-made decisions but the regional work must start from the wide diversity of local experiences.

At this gathering there is a feeling of pressure to reach conclusions and harmonize processes. In the actual preparation of the consultation regional considerations have been peripheral. Also, much of the planning has come from the North while we in the South have not been able to make it our own.

— Any process must be based on the principle of mutual trust. In a polarized and ideologized world ESR is not a wholly neutral field nor is it free from certain basic presuppositions. There are ideological tensions running through it. Likewise there is a variety of agendas and of approaches to problems. There can be no talk of trust unless we first of all confess our different motives and agendas.

— The principle of equality is more a desire than a reality. In our experience, for instance, the well-known system of evaluations is used to defend decisions which have already been taken. And it is right that we should be evaluated — but what about our right to evaluate what the agencies cooperating with us are doing in our region?

— Is it not utopian to talk about equality when one party is sharing their money and the other at most their dire poverty and their experiences?

— Resource-sharing automatically implies strengthening the ecumenical movement so that there can be a better chance of defining criteria and harmonizing principles when decisions are to be taken. This is the context in which the theme of bilateralism has to be placed. Sometimes bilateralism looks like an attempt to weaken the ecumenical effort and make it difficult to create real alternatives from the standpoint of the poor.

— Good intentions are not enough. There is a central problem: what are the mechanisms for establishing criteria or strategies in the sharing of resources? In the new guidelines we must prevent the mechanisms turning into means of intervention by those who really have the power.

— There is the problem of the neo-conservative offensive in the third-world countries. One of the biggest problems has its roots in the large sums of money coming into our countries in that way, and being used to promote work of a wholly different kind from ours. This theme is

not greatly stressed in resource-sharing but it is becoming one of central importance.
— The final document must be presented as something positive and not as negative injunctions telling people what must not be done.
— There is pessimism about whether a consultation has any real possibility of changing a system but the attempt is acknowledged to be a valid one. In practice there are extremely concrete problems which frustrate or hinder sharing in practice. The agencies often operate an agenda of their own and the result is the somewhat perturbing tendency to "open" offices in our countries. The WCC itself in our region is represented by work which is very much broken up among its various sub-units. Nor can we forget the local interests themselves, both of some churches and of certain groups.
El Escorial must be part of this conscientizing process on the basis of precise and clear guidelines.
— Any change in ESR must not compromise commitment to the people's movement. In our region the problem of the foreign debt and the burden it imposes on society must be one of the priorities for establishing criteria.
— There must be a break with the present system of evaluations and the regions must be helped to take on this task and take decisions themselves.
— The theme of the quincentenary of the Spanish Conquest should be one of the programmes to contribute to harmonizing criteria and efforts in the region.
— Generally speaking the proposed guidelines are considered to be positive, as are the possibilities of gradually establishing a new spirit in resource-sharing. Regional identities must figure more prominently and stress must be laid on the central importance of the third world and the poor in every aspect of this system. But unattainable utopias must be avoided.

Middle East
The reflections of the group were at two different levels: (1) broad concerns, and (2) organizational aspects of resource-sharing.

Broad concerns
The region is tense due to local problems and external intervention. The Christian presence is being eroded due to a variety of social and

economic factors. Rising fanaticism is a factor in the emigration of Christians.

International aid is swamping the Middle East. Careful screening is therefore necessary to decide on the reception of aid. External organizations which do not practise solidarity with the churches and Christians should not be encouraged to work in the region. The programmes and policies of diakonia of the churches and the external partners should reflect the priorities of pastoral care to the Christians.

There are not enough ecumenical projects in the region which are jointly undertaken by several churches. Future diakonia programmes should encourage such cooperative efforts. Construction projects are still important in the Middle East, for sustaining the community spirit and caring for young people in particular.

Organizational aspects

The Middle East will continue to need a regional group as a centre for decision-making on resource-sharing. In certain parts of the region it may be possible to establish national structures for this purpose, such as church councils or national councils. Regional and national structures should be complementary.

The basic principle is that local communities decide themselves on their project. Pre-screening at the local level should therefore be encouraged.

Both the regional ecumenical body (MECC) and the WCC have their role in the organization, coordination of resource-sharing structures in the region. The member churches of the two bodies must have a clear voice in it.

There is a need to clarify the function of the regional group with regard to comprehensive programmes such as country programmes and other major multilateral support structures for international aid in the region.

Special attention should be given to the participation of youth in decisions on resource-sharing. Young people should have more opportunities to attend ecumenical meetings and learn about ecumenism.

Local structures for promotion of loans for income-generating activities and housing should be encouraged.

North America

The North American group consisted of seven representatives from Canada and 18 representatives from the United States, in addition to two

WCC staff persons, four observers and one coopted staff person. The regional group had three major sessions.

The first session was devoted to becoming acquainted and discussing how the group should proceed with its work during the consultation. There was considerable discussion regarding the attempt to hold a preparatory meeting of the North American group in New York on 23 September 1987, which participants from Canada had decided not to attend, sensing that the agenda of the participants from the two nations would be very different. The US meeting on 23 September had commended the statement coming from a forum on ecumenical sharing of resources at a meeting of the unit committee of the Division of Overseas Ministries, NCCCUSA, in September 1986, as a fair statement of the perspective of the US churches. The final decision of the regional group was to meet together for the next session, but employing the "fishbowl" model, with the Canadian participants engaging in discussion while the US participants listened, and then vice versa. It also was decided, preparatory to the next session, to list the ways in which Canadian and US churches now actually are engaging in ecumenical sharing.

In the second session, the group engaged in the fishbowl process described above, with each group discussing concerns regarding the working document, general concerns, follow-up possibilities, and process questions. Following this process, it was agreed that two persons (one from Canada, one from the US) would draw together the input from this session and prepare a single document, which would serve as a resource for each member of the North American group in his/her working group discussions; it would also be presented to the plenary on behalf of this regional group.

The third session was devoted first to considering the report from the consultation's drafting committee. Comments were recorded for sharing with the drafting committee. Then the group discussed strategies for follow-up of this consultation, again employing the fishbowl process. A summary of this discussion follows.

Discussion among Canadian participants

What is the objective of the follow-up? To engage leadership of our churches and ecumenical agencies in both the experience and discussion of the message of this consultation on resource-sharing.

What cooperation should there be? Insofar as possible, Canadian and US participants should cooperate in planning follow-up.

We must see how our follow-up gets back into the life of local churches.

Plans were discussed for a travelling "roadshow" to the headquarters of each of the communions represented at this consultation (United Church of Canada, Anglican Church of Canada, Presbyterian Church of Canada) on 3 and 4 December 1987.

It was agreed to develop further plans for involving Canadian Council communions not represented at the consultation, especially the Lutheran and Roman Catholic churches.

It was agreed to seek an opportunity for a presentation at the triennial assembly of Canadian Council of Churches, on 7-12 May 1988 in Montreal, for which the theme is "Sharing of Gifts".

There was discussion of the problem of interpreting the consultation in western Canada, where the Canadian Council of Churches means little.

It was agreed to seek to have "Ten Days for Development" consider the topic of ecumenical sharing as a major emphasis.

There may be a need to decentralize our budgets so that follow-up can be carried out in the various regions of Canada, involving many volunteers.

There was discussion of the idea of some event, perhaps with US partners, bringing some persons from churches of the South to speak of their concerns. What can be the link between Canadian and US churches to carry out a back-to-back event, utilizing the same resource persons?

Discussion among US participants

It was agreed that the task before us is to get the major decision-makers of communions and ecumenical agencies informed, conscientized, and motivated to act on the basic concept articulated by this consultation.

There is need for a specific event to get the decision-makers together, along with representatives of partners from the churches of the South.

Where to begin? The US resource-sharing committee could be the locus around which such an event might be convened, along with US commissioners serving on various WCC commissions.

We need to recreate this kind of experience, including worship, Bible study, etc., and not be limited to bureaucrat-to-bureaucrat conversations.

There is need to communicate these priorities to our individual communions, both through official communications and personal contact.

We should try to get our own boards to subscribe to these principles, coming to the discussion with colleagues from other churches who have shared in this experience.

We should also seek to involve independent grant-making bodies within our churches, e.g. United Thank Offering (Episcopal), Presbyterian Hunger Program, etc.

Other key persons and groups need to be informed and involved, e.g. bishops, executive councils, mission divisions, education commissions, multi-cultural ministries, women's councils, etc.

There is a need to build a sense of solidarity across the divided structures within our churches and ecumenical agencies, involving all people in their diversity of race, gender, class, age, communion, helping us to get over those things that keep us apart.

The culminating event should be regional, inclusive of both Canada and the USA.

Following these two periods of discussion, there was time for only a brief discussion in which it was agreed that the Canadian and US follow-up groups would stay in touch with each other, looking towards the possibility of a single or sequential follow-up event(s) in late 1988.

Pacific

The group looked at the report of the Pacific pre-consultation and emphasized the following points concerning: (1) the concept of ecumenical sharing, and (2) the mechanisms.

The concept

Ecumenical sharing of resources is of particular relevance for the region because it can build on and give new life to the existing pattern of cultural sharing and extend it beyond its traditional limits. It is an expression of Christian commitment.

The relationships of the Pacific churches are mostly bilateral and denominational, locally as well as internationally. Yet sharing among churches is possible and can start in small ways in each local situation.

The Pacific Conference of Churches and the national councils of churches have an important role in promoting ecumenical sharing in the region. The churches could be asked to set aside their offering on a special day for ecumenical work at the national and regional level. The PCC could facilitate the sharing of human resources by enabling people from different Pacific countries to take part in workshops on particular concerns organized by a local church or a national council.

Ongoing dialogue between the churches is basic to the sharing of resources, because of the varying responses churches make on social and political issues, e.g. decolonization, nuclear and other justice issues in the region. Only through dialogue can the churches in the Pacific region reach mutual understanding in different political contexts.

Visits are an important means to enable communication between the churches on issues of concern and to share spiritual and material resources with one another. Existing denominational patterns of visitation can be expanded to encourage ecumenical sharing and dialogue.

Theological and spiritual sharing can be deepened by:
— making biblical reflection an integral part of all gatherings;
— developing a Pacific prayer cycle for use in all the churches;
— strengthening the ecumenical communication among groups like youth, women, pastors, etc.

Financial sharing among the churches in the region is minimal. There are a few examples of solidarity expressed through small material or financial contributions in the case of disasters, but most of the projects in the Pacific are largely dependent on funding from outside the region. It is difficult for many Pacific people to understand the "systems" whereby resources especially from overseas are made available. Many of these systems require particular reporting and conditions to be met. Obviously the local churches should be assisted to understand the systems of ecumenical sharing and stewardship responsibilities. WCC/CICARWS and the PCC should be able to facilitate such information-sharing and training which will strengthen the understanding and stewardship involved in sharing ecumenically, including developing personnel resources.

The people in the Pacific have always been receiving from outside whatever is given, even with conditions. Pacific people must learn to say *no*, if what is given is not to the best interest of the whole people or for the region as a whole. We have the power to make the decision. Power can only be shared if people are allowed to participate. Power should not be mishandled or misused, it should be used for the best interests of all people. The churches should empower people for self-determination, making their own decisions, and deciding for the life of the whole community.

Financial aid from richer countries can only be of real value to the Pacific if it does not contribute to widening the gap between the haves and the have-nots.

The involvement of para-church organizations in the region is a major factor which requires special attention.

The mechanisms

The Pacific advisory group should be more widely representative. The francophone group, Melanesia, Polynesia, Marshalls/Micronesia, PCC secretariat, WCC-CICARWS, and funding partners should be represented.

Each of these groupings is expected to meet independently to discuss their own agenda and to make recommendations to the PAG.

A round table meeting should be organized as a pre-Assembly meeting of the PCC to look at issues in the Pacific in light of Assembly directives and see what progress has been made, to learn from each other what the PCC, the NCCs and the constituent bodies are doing, to learn about PAG and PCC/WCC relationships, etc. This meeting would involve church leaders, women, youth, NCC representatives, together with mission boards, funding partners and WCC.

The PAG should not only be concerned with sharing of material resources but also of personnel within the region and worldwide as well. It should serve as a board of mission for the region under guidelines mutually agreed upon by PCC/WCC and funding partners.

The group then considered the first draft of the proposed discipline and made the following comments.

Ecumenical sharing in its biblical context should begin with sharing Christ. The experiences of Christian communities of living and growing in Christ should be shared with others. Then sharing in the eucharist, in mission, financial sharing and other forms of sharing should follow.

Ecumenical sharing is a basis of our commitment, mission and life. It is not a special department within the structures of our churches. Therefore, ecumenical relationships begin at home, between and among local churches. Old divisions and differences tend to become barriers of ecumenism, so the call to repentance is vitally important as a part of our commitment.

The issue of nuclear testing and dumping of nuclear waste in the Pacific should be part of the commitment to confront the root causes of injustice.

Inter-regional meeting (of representatives from Africa, Asia, Caribbean, Latin America, Middle East, Pacific)

The following remarks were made with regard to the proposed discipline:

That all the points in the code of discipline are to be taken as an entirety, not separately.

Issues should include foreign debt, self-reliance, respect, and the recognition of popular people's movements for liberation and justice.

We should take serious note of oppressive systems on the global, regional and national levels.

We in the South will not receive money from churches and agencies who are not in solidarity with us in our people's struggles. We call on the North to address issues that affect the South in their own contexts.

Some feedback:

The self-emptying, suffering Jesus should be held up and the theological dimension strengthened and sharpened.

The structures of inequality and domination have to be studied, and the contradictions that these generate identified in the document.

The whole issue of ecumenical sharing of resources has to be understood within the perspectives of power, which is a political issue.

Serious attention must be given to strengthening South-to-South relationships in all of the disciplines.

The WCC should address the global community on issues that impinge on the process of resource-sharing.

One World

In our prayers today we celebrate the one world — the oneness of the human family that transcends the barriers of race, class, colour, religions, etc.
We shall celebrate this oneness in acts of intercession and praise.
But let us first pray for strength to transcend our own limitations and ask for forgiveness because often we have forgotten that the earth and all its fullness belongs to the Lord.

Let us pray.

Eternal God, you are the author of life; all living beings depend on you; you care for all the earth.
We pray for our neighbours whose expressions of faith or convictions are different from ours; the longings of whose hearts we do not always comprehend.
Teach us to know that you love all peoples.
Help us to respect what we do not yet understand and to rejoice in the words and acts of truth, beauty and love, wherever they may be found.
Enable us to love others as you love and to live with others in ways that build your loving rule over all of life.
We ask this in the name of him who gave himself for all, Jesus Christ, our Lord. Amen.

People (sung response)
"Break down the walls that separate us
and unite us in a single body"   (see following page)

Fred Kaan/Peter Janssens

Break down the walls that se- par- ra -te us and u-

nite us in a sin-gle bo- dy

bo- dy.

Leader
Eternal God, free us from fear and prejudice; free us from the ignorance
that holds us back from rejoicing that we belong to the one human family.
Set us free to belong and to care.

People (sung response)

Leader
Loving God, free us from narrowness of mind
that is too quick to reject, from self-righteousness
that is too ready to judge, from smallness of spirit
that fails to see the good in others.
Set us free to love and learn.

People (sung response)

Leader
Merciful God, free us from our hesitation to witness to your love,
our unwillingness to listen to the witness of others,
our slowness to discern you in places we least expect.
Set us free to perceive and to believe.

Bible Studies

CHRISTOPHER DURAISINGH

Introduction

There are several ways of looking at the Bible for insights on our theme. The traditional way is to look at various biblical stories about sharing, such as the widow's mite, the feeding of the five thousand, or at more narrative passages on giving, such as those in 2 Corinthians 9, etc. But what I want to do in these days is to select three key concepts in the Bible and to examine, both individually and in inter-relation, how they bring out relevant insights on sharing in and for a world community in Christ.

The three concepts are *covenant, body, eucharist*. Each of these three concepts is pregnant with enormous possibilities for our consideration. But, more importantly, each contributes to and enriches our understanding of the other. For example, the concept of "covenant" raises crucial issues for sharing, but as a model in itself it tends to become arbitrary or contractual, for it is often used in a managerial or organizational sense. The metaphor "body" with its organic connotations therefore adds to and corrects the pitfalls of the "covenant" concept as a model for sharing. But it, too, in itself may lack the purposefulness and spontaneous commitment which is so crucial in koinonia based on the love of God in Jesus Christ shed abroad in our hearts by the power of the Holy Spirit. It is here that the "eucharist" — where the *body* is *broken* and the *blood of the covenant* is poured out — is a bringing together of both these concepts.

It is interesting that the motifs of "body" and "covenant" are essential parts of eucharistic theology in the Bible. I therefore want us to look at these concepts not only in themselves but in their relationship to each other, thus enabling us to gain a more holistic understanding of sharing life in and for a world community in Christ.

I. Covenant as a subversive paradigm for sharing life in community

Leviticus 26:9-13; 25:8-13,23-28; Acts 4:32-35

Why use the term "subversive" (Walter Bruggemann's phrase)? What is the significance of the concept of the covenant in the Old Testament? It is subversive in many aspects. I will identify three of them.

First, it subverts our understanding of God. Two distinct understandings of God can often be identified: (1) God as one who — out of God's generosity — gives, and hence sharing is an extra, optional for God; (2) the other speaks of sharing life as definitional of God — i.e. apart from God's continuous sharing of life with the whole of creation there is no way of knowing or speaking about the God of the Bible. In this sense, the concept of "covenant" puts a question mark against a bourgeois understanding of a God who gives out of God's plenitude without pain or hurt to self. Here, then, is a concept of God which defines God in and through the act of God's covenant relationship with humankind.

Second, those who are involved in the sharing of the covenant are *habirus* — those who are not related to the powerful, not the landed people but the nomads and nobodies of society. Covenant partners with God are those who are at the underside of history.

Third, sharing within the covenant relationship does not dwell upon the movement from a stronger to the weaker partner as we often tend to interpret it. The primary emphasis is rather upon the solidarity and total availability of each to the other. This means there is a refusal to make sharing manageable. The very purpose of covenant is the maximum guarantee of the wholeness of every member of the covenant community and therefore there is a constant refusal to reduce the covenant into manageable laws and rules. To speak of "rules" of the covenant is an aberration, and the prophets constantly fight such a reductionistic tendency.

Partners in sharing

One significant aspect of all concepts — particularly religious concepts — and images, is the *self-understanding* of the community through that concept. In this sense, covenant describes essentially what the community of sharing was, and who were the tribes. What is the sociological function of the act fulfilled? Norman Gottwald is helpful here. Hence the identity of the partners becomes significant. Leviticus 25 and 26 give us the clue that these were immigrants, landless refugees — the *habirus*. They were the opposite of the inhabitants of the land — the landed aristocracy, those who had a place, who held power and authority. Only those who recognize that they are all equally *habirus*, the nobodies, can be truly bonded together. Christian sharing does not mean from the "haves" to the "have-nots". There is no room either for the language or the mind-set represented in the "donor-receiver" structures we are accustomed to. Nor is there room for the language of "grant" as given by the North to the South. Sharing in the covenant mode presupposes acknowledgment of "empty hands" on both sides. We are called here to a metanoia, an alteration of mind-sets, for nothing less than repentance and a conversion from the mind-set of "haves" and "have-nots" will do. People who are tied to cultures or economies that are too triumphalistic and powerful cannot share. For, undergirding the community of the covenant, there is a common memory of oppression, a common praxis against the landed aristocracy, a common hope of inheriting together the promised land.

The initiative is God's

But what is the nature of the God of the covenant? Hosea, one of the earliest prophets to use extensively the motif of "covenant", presents God as one who breaks all stereotype images. Certainly Hosea's God is not portrayed by a male-macho image, but rather as a God of pathos, of passion; a God who can agonize in the anguish of the covenant-partners. As Bruggemann puts it, this is a God who refuses to play god, the almighty, the all-sufficient and self-contained. Rather, this God expresses a need for love and for a relationship. Sharing is *not* optional. Nor does this God come to the covenant relation with all the questions already answered. God is open through and through, taken advantage of and cheated, yet remains in constant relationship. Here we have the image of a relational God: everything is at stake for the covenanting God who lets self become exposed and impinged upon. The image of the God of the covenant is set over against images of a God who moves only from power. The name of this God is Yahweh, "I will be what I will be" — an action word; God as verb, futuristic, open-minded.

The nature of sharing involved in the covenant model

The role of meal and of the mingling of blood signifies a mingling and interpenetration of selves, of the lives and histories of the covenant partners; it involves an internal structural alteration in the lives of the partners and not merely an external contract or cool negotiation, a scientific process of objectively "screening" projects in the way that "donor" agencies are prone to do. Nothing less than a redefinition of self within the "sharing" process can bring about a community, a new humanity.

Covenant relationship even subverts the very question we are asking at this conference — how do we share? The very notion of "sharing" is questioned, for it implies that we already possess something that we can now share. But look at Leviticus, and particularly at the Jubilee injunctions that are given to keep the covenant relationship true to its purpose (Lev. 25). The question here is not simply what and how we share, but rather to whom does what we seek to share belong? In the final analysis, it is not sharing that the Jubilee is calling for but rather for a radical restructuring; not "sharing" but "reparation"; not new principles of sharing but a just restructuring of relationships so that a new beginning is guaranteed for all. But if it is neither donor-centred nor recipient-centred, to whom does it belong? It belongs to God. It is a reordering of the institutions of covenant; any other starting place is sinful. Ecumenical sharing of resources (ESR) is the transfer of wealth back to the original owners.

If you look at Acts 2, and 4:32-35, the early Christians did not give out of surplus but dipped into their capital: see also Exodus 22:25-ff. (v.25: "If you advance money to any poor man amongst my people you shall not act like a money-lender: you must not exact interest in advance from him"). This is a contrast between the law of the land and what is just. The logic of divine economy and the logic of the world become different. On the question of land distribution, more than 60% of the land in the world is in the hands of 20% of the world's people. There is a clear understanding of persons over property, public concern over private, faithfulness over success; the community benefits over the few. The goal of sharing is shalom, justice and peace. In Jeremiah 22:13-17, knowledge, love and worship of God are shalom- and justice-oriented.

The same emphasis continues in the Gospels, but something new is added. The essential thrust is not in selling and giving away, but on a new order of human community, a new quality of relationship which is worthy of the kingdom of God, cf. Luke 10, the good Samaritan; Mark 10:29-30:
— v.17: "... what must I do to win eternal life?";
— v.25: "It is easier for a camel to pass through the eye of a needle than for a rich man to enter the kingdom of God";
— v.28-31: "At this Peter spoke. 'We here', he said, 'have left everything to become your followers'. Jesus said, 'I tell you this: there is no one who has given up home, brothers or sisters, mother, father or children, or land, for my sake and for the Gospel, who will not

receive in this age a hundred times as much — houses, brothers and sisters, mothers and children, and land — and persecutions besides; and in the age to come eternal life. But many who are first will be last and the last first.'"

One word is missing in the parallelism — "fathers": patriarchism is clearly given up with the new order. Also, Matthew 23:9 instructs us to call only God "Father": a new relationship of unlimited liability — total availability. Ananias and Sapphira did not understand that (Acts 5). The unexpected dropping in of guests is a totally new kind of relationship (Rom. 12:13, Heb. 13:2). The Good Samaritan story never tells us what happened to the victim but only what happened to the good Samaritan — to whom can you become a neighbour? You have to go through a life alteration by altering your life-style; thus the Samaritan transforms into a neighbour. The giving of resources is not important; what *is* important is the willingness to redefine self in terms of the other.

Isaiah 19:23 — within covenant sharing, Israel and Egypt are connected, a highway is established as a blessing and as a light to the nations. Dangers here include: (1) a tendency to reduce covenant into a neat, manageable and workable formula; a covenant turned into a contract; the prophets fight against this time and again; (2) the introversion of the covenant model in a small community; (3) theology develops, the indestructability of Zion. God is a God of the covenant; conventional images of God are not appropriate.

II. Body as a liberating metaphor for sharing life in community

2 Corinthians 12:12-31; Romans 12:4-8; Ephesians 4:1-13

If in the Old Testament the most common paradigm is "covenant", in the New Testament the most predominant one is *body* — an organic metaphor. Again in the Old Testament we find the "community of the covenant", while in the New Testament the people of God are the body of Christ. The two models are functionally and structurally different. It is important to see the distinction between them as well as their unique contribution; together they complement each other in throwing light upon our search for relevant model(s) for sharing life in community.

The biblical use of the term "body" seeks to break open this "natural" and "organic" static metaphor and to present it with an eschatological purpose and potency. This is so because of the active association of the Spirit of God and the body; the people of God become the body of Christ in the Spirit. We find the clue in 1 Corinthians 12: the outgoing, sharing

Spirit of God constitutes the body and makes it dynamic. If "covenant" is grounded in the outgoing love of God, the body is grounded in the outgoing Spirit of God. In the next study we shall observe that the eucharist, our third concept, is grounded in the self-giving love of the Son in the power of the Spirit to the glory of God, the parent.

It is this grounding in the Spirit that makes all the difference: the church is not just a body, but the body of Christ, the Messiah, the Sent One; God's shared life — a liberated metaphor. What is shared is love, while everything else is secondary. The gifts that any part of the body has are the charismata — the gifts of the Spirit. Everything we have is given to us by the Spirit; nothing is natural to us; there is a building up of the people of God as living stones. The whole body is not simply the sum of its parts but has to be looked at as a whole. The giver-receiver model does not suffice, for neither North nor South can be identified on its own. Diversity exists, but only insofar as it is appropriate for a living organism — the body. It is when any member tries to ground itself totally in itself that disease develops and destroys the body. "You are, I know, eager for gifts of the Spirit; then aspire above all to excel in those which build up the church" — the edification of the church (1 Cor. 14:12).

"Because I am not a... , I do not belong to the body" (1 Cor. 12:14ff.): to say that is to deny the wholeness of the body. Sometimes we say this without being aware that we are doing so; the moment need is expressed, there is silence. By not using things from other churches in our worship services, we are *de facto* saying "No, I don't need you" — we are monochrome. Verses 23 and 24 liberate the model from hierarchy: v.22-26:

> Quite the contrary: those organs of the body which seem to be more frail than others are indispensable, and those parts of the body which we regard as less honourable are treated with special honour. To our unseemly parts is given a more than ordinary seemliness, whereas our seemly parts need no adorning. But God has combined the various parts of the body, giving special honour to the humbler parts, so that there might be no sense of division in the body, but that all its organs might feel the same concern for one another. If one organ suffers, they all suffer together. If one flourishes, they all rejoice together.

Re-evaluation and an inversion of values is called for: those that are the weakest are to be valued more. Jesus was disposed to this inversion of values: in Samuel 5:8-9 the blind and the crippled cannot enter; in Matthew 21:14 Jesus inverts that.

What then are the implications for resource-sharing? The first is that we need to bring the periphery to the centre, for asymmetry can only arrange itself through hierarchy. Peter Ruge, author of *Ministry and Management,* says that most churches that adopt the "body" model do structure themselves in a hierarchical way. So we must ask whose culture our decision-making structures represent: do our decisions create a power structure with a class of elitists? Galatians 3:28 affirms that "there is no such thing as Jew and Greek, slave and freeman, male and female; for you are all one person in Jesus Christ". Romans 12:5 also states that each member belongs to all the others: "So all of us, united with Christ, form one body, serving individually as limbs and organs to one another."

Ephesians 4:16 teaches us that it is not a bilateral but a multilateral relationship which exists when each member belongs to all: "He is the head and on him the whole body depends. Bonded and knit together by every constituent joint, the whole frame grows through the due activity of each part, and builds itself up in love." 1 Corinthians 12:25 emphasizes the mutuality of such relationships within the body: "… so that there might be no sense of division in the body, but that all its organs might feel the same concern for one another". This phrase "one another" — a powerful expression in the Bible — occurs at least 28 times in various manifestations: "admonishing one another", "bear one another's burdens", "serve one another".

A second implication is that resources need to be assimilated — resources accumulated by one belong to all, perhaps stored by one for awhile. Using the "body" image, we see that the North has been functioning like the stomach. We know what happens when too much food stays in the stomach for a long time: one becomes ill. The crisis of capitalism is a symptom of the deeper illness; to invest and hold capital will cause the stomach to ache. But it is through sharing that growth and healing take place.

Such sharing must take place in all aspects of relationship, for when one member suffers, all members suffer. "If one organ suffers, they all suffer together. If one flourishes, they all rejoice together" (1 Cor. 12:26). Such sharing implies solidarity at all costs. We must not be misled into thinking that suffering is powerlessness; rather, it is the suffering of the cross that explodes all power systems. One Hebrew word for compassion is womb. This suggests that we cannot share resources unless there is body pain. Therefore, it is not decision-making but pain-bearing that forms and informs the relationship of resource-sharing.

Finally, the metaphor of the "body" is stretched beyond its limits and made eschatalogical: "He is, moreover, the head of the body, the church; he is its origin, the first to return from the dead, to be in all things alone supreme" (Col. 1:18-20). Also, "(the God of our Lord Jesus Christ)... has made him the supreme head of the church, which is his body and as such holds within it the fullness of him who himself receives the entire fullness of God" (Eph. 1:22-23).

III. Eucharist as a holistic and costly model for sharing life in community

Exodus 24:7-11; 1 Corinthians 11:22-33; Isaiah 25:6-8; Matthew 8:11; John 13:1-20

The eucharist is a potential holistic model for the common sharing of life, for in it are brought together the two motifs of "covenant" and "body".

Frustrations have been expressed about the use of the eucharist as a model for the ecumenical sharing of resources, because the eucharist is the one act of the church that divides and excludes. However, it is precisely because of the division and exclusion it causes that it *is* the model.

First of all, let us consider the aspect of division. 1 Corinthians 11:17ff. shows the eucharist to be the one event that can bring people together and break open the body to bring people in. This passage has three sections, and between the two sections of division comes the eucharist.

Second, regarding exclusion, we must remember that the initial intention of the eucharist is evangelistic mission: "Do this in remembrance". The body is broken and blood is shed in order that wholeness can be given to the many — an inverted inclusiveness. It is in the eucharist that the church renews itself (1 Cor. 11:23-33; John 13:1-20).

There are three points to be considered in the general understanding of the eucharistic paradigm. First there is the centrality of feasting, of eating, to this event. In the post-resurrection narratives, it is in eating and drinking that we see Jesus. Acts 10:40-41 records that the risen Lord was seen only by those who ate and drank with him: "... but God raised him to life on the third day, and allowed him to appear, not to the whole people, but to witnesses whom God had chosen in advance — to us, who ate and drank with him after he rose from the dead." Immediately after Pentecost, the central act of the church is the breaking of bread. In addition, a large number of Jesus' parables about the kingdom have to do with banquets. Eating and drinking is a most powerful paradigm for sharing life; it gives a new identity to the church, a new covenant in one body.

Secondly, the Last Supper is situated between two noted points — the past and the future. It is preceded by table fellowship with sinners and publicans, while at the same time looking towards the final promised banquet of the kingdom when all God's children will sit at the table and be satisfied (this is referred to in several instances in all three Synoptic Gospels, including Matthew 8:11). So it is with us: we too are looking backwards as well as forward. Therefore the eucharist is a paradigm for where we are.

Third, the eucharistic paradigm provides a relationship between covenant and body. In the eucharist there is the affirmation of covenant and body which are brought together in a dynamic way, and, at the same time, incarnation and atonement are brought together. Through the eucharist the static metaphor of "body" is made organic — a new covenant in one body.

In John 13:1-20 we find the Johannine parallel of the Lord's Supper. Here is provided the precondition, the preposture for the eucharist; here we see the necessary posture, preparatory for eucharistic sharing. This is one of the most powerful sections of the Bible, for here we have the affirmation that Jesus loves us to the end. The previous section talks about *logos,* while here it moves to pathos — passion, loving. Unless we move away from law, we cannot move towards love.

This passage also implies the power of divesting. "Jesus, well aware that the Father had entrusted everything to him, and that he had come from God and was going back to God, rose from the table, laid aside his garments, and taking a towel, tied it round him" (John 13:3-4). Knowing that all power is given to you, the outer garment can be taken off. The moment you know you have the resources, divesting can begin.

Thus we see the eucharist as a critique of the logic of the system. The towel and basin — two symbols which are authentic marks for resource-sharing — are the focus at the climax of this passage. With them, Jesus takes on the identity of a servant, an identity which is given in terms of the person being served. It is not humility that is called for, but vulnerability — total vulnerability. Jesus assumes a servant posture in taking a towel. We are reminded of a similar action in the Pharisee's house in Luke 7:44: "Then, turning to the woman, he said to Simon, 'You see this woman? I came to your house: you provided no water for my feet; but this woman has made my feet wet with her tears and wiped them with her hair.'" These passages reflect a structural posture that hurts, that appears to be impractical; the posture of washing someone's feet makes one maximally sensitive and maximally available. It is a posture which can participate authentically in the structures of resource-sharing.

Let us look also at 1 Corinthians 11:17ff. This passage is in three parts (vv.17-22; 23-27; 28-34). Here, the eucharist is placed in the context of social praxis, social relationship. It is a critique of the current practice of resource-sharing which is set in the context of the swollen appetites of a few while others are deprived. They were embarrassed; private interests become institutionalized, sacralized.

Between the two sections comes the eucharist, beginning with the devastating comment: "on the night when he was betrayed". The eucharist is through and through a political action. The body of Christ is broken. The Lord's Supper is charged as an act of treason.

Verses 24-25 portray Jesus taking bread and offering it up to God in thanks. Not in the same way as we give thanks; rather, it is the holding up of the whole body as an offering to God — a total offering up of ourselves. Thus, offering up, breaking and sharing are the three decisive parts to the model. The Corinthians missed this; they thought the purpose was to keep it, to eat, while the real purpose was to break it, to break it open.

"For he who eats and drinks eats and drinks judgment on himself if he does not discern the Body. That is why many of you are feeble and sick, and a number have died" (vv.29-30). If you do not recognize and discern the body, you will be ill. "Body" most probably refers to the community. Thus if you do not discern the nature of the community (the sick, the poor, etc), you are sick.

The eucharistic elements — the bread and the wine — identify for us the ordinary bread and wine made by ordinary people. Together they represent a conclusion that there can be no separation between the material and the spiritual. They are some of the most ordinary things, and through them the periphery comes to the centre to bring about a radical shift in the paradigm. The labour of all the people is brought together here: the poor who crushed the wine; the crushed body. It is an inclusive model: it is the world which now becomes Christ's body.

What is significant in this passage is the verbs. There are at least seven verbs, of which the main one is *breaking*. The meaning of the model is found in the brokenness and in being broken. First, you are broken; you are naked, transparent and available to be seen. The second is a broken structure for the many, where the centre becomes the outside and the periphery moves to the centre. Third is the power represented in the brokenness. This power is the victory *of* the cross, not *over* the cross. The way of the cross is the way of ultimate reality — the way of justice, of love, and of sharing.

One Light

Leader
Eternal God, dispel the darkness of war and violence and shed on the
nations the light of peace.

Orthodox liturgy, USSR

Leader
Loving God, remove the darkness of ignorance and self-love and shed on
your peoples the light of love.

People
Kyrie eleison

Leader
Living God, defeat the darkness of evil and death and shed on the earth
the light of life.

People
Kyrie eleison

Leader
Gracious God, cast out the darkness of fear and suspicion and shed on us
the light of hope.

People
Kyrie eleison

Leader
Eternal God,
You have called us to be the children of light
and have taught us that those who do not love their
brother and sister, dwell in darkness —
May the time that we have together at this consultation
shed light on who we are and how we share.
May the light of life that we see in the life of Christ,
that was shared with the poor, the oppressed and the
rejected of his time, dispel our ignorance and blindness;
May the light of your word, the lamp unto our feet,
guide us in the commitments we will make at this meeting
And hasten the time when the fullness of glory will fill
the earth and the nations walk in your light.

People
Kyrie eleison

Leader
Living God, teach us not to be afraid of darkness,
but enable us to overcome it.
For —
there was darkness over the earth before creation,
there was darkness in the womb before birth,
there was darkness in the tomb before resurrection.

   (silence)

Testimonies

The consultation was an occasion to tell and to listen to each other's stories, testimonies, perspectives; sometimes also anger and frustrations. Some of that was included in the programme, much happened spontaneously. Only a few of these are included in this report. They reflect something of the diversity of experiences and expectations; their inclusion here is an invitation to continue the "story-telling" as an essential element of the commitment "to represent to one another our needs and problems in relationships where there are no absolute donors, or absolute recipients, but all have needs to be met and gifts to give, and to work for the structural changes in the institutions of the North and the South which this calls for".

Egypt: a round-table experience

I am pleased to share with you all one of our experiences of ecumenical resource-sharing. It is the experience of the round-table programme of the Coptic Orthodox Church in Egypt.

The Coptic Orthodox Church is the largest church in the Middle East. The membership is about 7 million. There are 34 dioceses. The round-table programme is a partnership of the Coptic Orthodox Church and 15 supporting ecumenical agencies of different denominations and from different countries.

The programme started in 1985. It covers the following areas: leadership training, employment generation, health education, youth-related activities, women and development, rural development education (literacy programme) and services to inaccessible groups.

Experiences acquired: After about two years of implementation of the programme, the following experiences have been acquired:
— The programme has enabled 34 dioceses of the church to share their resources and coordinate their activities. A more equitable distribu-

tion of resources has been achieved. In the past the project system has been an experience of fragmentation of diakonia. The church is now able to set up a long-term plan according to the real needs of the people.

— At local level there is more cooperation between the programme activities and the activities of other churches.

— At national level two ecumenical seminars for leadership training were conducted in cooperation with the Coptic evangelical organization for development and the Upper Egypt Catholic Association. In cooperation with Caritas Egypt, the programme has started a training course for people working with the mentally handicapped.

— At international level the programme is a humble instrument for ecumenical sharing of resources. Fifteen agencies from different countries and denominations are learning how to share their resources with the Coptic Orthodox Church in a spirit of solidarity and partnership. These two years have taught us that this is not an easy task.

— The programme has begun to enable the partners to know and understand each other. It is also an opportunity for agencies to work together in a certain programme. On the other hand, it helps to balance the situation of the church with the mandates of the agencies.

The programme has faced some challenges:

— Trust is the basis of the relationship between us and the supporting partners. Building trust needs efforts from both sides.

— We are beginning to learn to share our weakness as well as our strength with our partners from abroad.

— We have pastoral needs and development needs; we are trying to integrate the two concepts.

— We are learning how we can serve our Coptic community of some 7 million people and be relevant to the larger societies.

— We are learning how to meet the growing needs of the communities in Egypt and at the same time deepen the quality of the church.

This month's meeting was a good experience of the round-table programme discussion and field visits to build a spirit of solidarity, to assess our services critically and to go beyond obsession with funds and financial accountability.

The partnership has moved from short-term commitment to long-term commitment as the result of growing trust on our side and on our partners' side.

Bishop Serapion

Cuba: an example of South-South sharing

Since 1981 the Ecumenical Council of Cuba has been participating in a project supporting the people of Kampuchea. Other participants in this project are Church World Service (NCCCUSA), the WCC, the Mennonite Central Committee (USA and Canada), and some churches in Canada and the Federal Republic of Germany. These organizations have provided the funds, while the Cuban churches have provided the human resources, i.e. the personnel. The project aims at helping the Kampuchean people to develop their agriculture, in particular the irrigation system and cattle breeding.

Until now twelve Cubans, young men and women, have taken part in the project, working there for one, two or three years. These young Cuban technicians are hydraulic engineers and veterinarians; they belong to the Presbyterian, Methodist, Baptist, Anglican and Evangelical Independent Churches.

At this very moment (October 1987) there are three Christian Cuban technicians at work, and two others — one hydraulic engineer from the Anglican church and an engineer in mechanics from the Evangelical Church of the New Pinetrees — are preparing themselves to join the project.

We believe that this is a good example of how a poor country of the third world can share its resources with another poor country which is also of the third world. In this sharing, the Christian Cuban technicians not only give through their knowledge and work, but also receive through the experiences, the suffering, the commitment and the life of the Kampuchean people.

Orestes Gonzalez Cruz

German Democratic Republic: what ecumenical sharing means for the churches

Ecumenical sharing takes place at various levels and in various directions, for example: within the churches; with other countries in Eastern Europe (see report of the Sofia consultation, May 1982); between many congregations in our country and in the Netherlands.

The significance of our relationships with churches in the so-called third world is growing. I can only point to some aspects and orientations.

In the past our churches were almost exclusively recipient churches, which has resulted in a widespread receiver mentality. This has been questioned and discussed for some years now. In particular, the GDR participants in the Melbourne conference on world mission (1980) brought these questions home. The ecumenical movement has helped us a lot to realize and to develop our own possibilities. Important stages in this learning process were the Church and Society conference (Geneva 1966), the WCC's Fourth Assembly in Uppsala in 1968 and the formation of our own church federation (i.e. independent from West Germany). Among the major challenges for the churches and the Christians were the Programme to Combat Racism and the call for a church in solidarity with the poor. From the beginning we have seen ecumenical sharing of resources as an important aspect of this challenge to be a church in solidarity with the poor, and also as part of the conciliar process (JPIC). I want to mention three ways in which we try to respond to these complex challenges.

1. Our efforts to build awareness, at all levels of the churches. This means not only to identify the root causes, the symptoms and the consequences of existing injustices, but much more to stimulate the congregations to engage in active solidarity, in the sense of co-responsibility and involvement.

2. Our efforts to link the whole programme of sharing to what we see as an effective "tool": the 2% Appeal. The acceptance of the 2% Appeal by many congregations, districts and regional churches is a visible expression of the seriousness of our endeavours to take part in the WCC programme of ecumenical sharing.

3. The search for new and wider forms of international and ecumenical diakonia and sharing. We have to take into account that our country does not have a freely convertible currency, and that we need the permission of our government for everything that has to do with international exchange of persons or transfer of goods. In this regard we may say that the authorities are more and more receptive to the concerns of the churches, something for which we are grateful.

Some of these new and wider forms of sharing are:
— the sending of personnel and the expansion of the scholarships programme;
— the development of long-term projects of the type "Helping to bring self-reliance", in cooperation with the churches or national councils in the receiving countries;
— the transformation of the old mission relationships into real partnerships;
— the challenge to our congregations to be open in their relations with foreigners who have come to our country for training;

— the exchange of experiences with national Christian councils in countries of the third world which have opted for a "non-capitalist" development;
— partnerships with congregations or groups in countries of the third world and with students from those countries.

We see our contribution to the programme of ecumenical sharing on the whole as rather modest, and we are also aware that we have not yet fully explored all the opportunities within our special context. The challenge is real, and we will continue to face it.

D. Graewe

Canada: signs of renewal

The sins committed by donor agencies in the past are known: imposition of criteria, expectations without dialogue, the implied superiority of the benefactor, etc. I hope that we can put both terms "donor" and "recipient" behind us and that, instead, the word "partners" can get more than lip service.

In the Canadian context there are some signs of renewal. Both the United Church and the Anglican Church of Canada have merged their mission and service departments in order to diminish divisions and to be able to relate in a more holistic way to their partners. The UCC and the Presbyterian Church have supported initiatives of South-South exchange, for example between Africa and China, and between Guyana and India. Much of the important work of the churches in Canada is done ecumenically. In our multicultural society with many denominations and a relatively small population, the churches are trying to respond together, both domestically and internationally, to issues of concern. The Inter-Church Fund for International Development (ICFID), for example, was established twelve years ago as a joint effort of the Roman Catholic, Lutheran, United, Anglican, Presbyterian and Mennonite churches, to bring an ecumenical witness to project funding. After a consultation with project representatives in 1979 it was decided to have three overseas board members. Since then other consultations have taken place, in particular with Latin American partners of ICFID. The most recent development of partnership is with Christian Care in Zimbabwe. The solution of overseas board members is not perfect: it has not yet resulted in real equality (financial constraints), it puts heavy demands on the persons appointed, and until now no woman has been appointed from overseas.

But messages have been heard and are taken seriously: "Tell Canadians the story. Make them understand their responsibility for world issues, what concerned Christians must do." Educational coalitions try to do this, for instance the Inter-Church Committees on Africa and on World Development Education, the latter better known as "Ten Days for World Development". Each year in late January the congregations are asked to focus on development issues in preparation for Lent. This has nothing to do with fund raising, but everything with people and solidarity. Visiting speakers from overseas do Canada (at an exhausting pace...), speaking to local groups who must be ecumenical. Other ecumenical coalitions concentrate on issues such as refugees, human rights in Latin America. Gattfly is a coalition working on economic justice and the international debt crisis; it has done a lot on the rights of sugar workers, which has led to the creation of the International Committee for Solidarity and Action of Sugar Workers. Project Ploughshares deals with issues of peace, disarmament and development. There is also a Task Force on Corporate Responsibility.

All these are small steps. But they point in the right direction.

Jean Davidson

Asia: a regional perspective

I am encouraged to dwell more on the positive side — the progress we have made in this area. Our Asia regional meeting once again reaffirmed our comprehensive understanding of resources. It is not just material alone — of which we have very little — but it includes spirituality, culture, human and similar resources.

Having said this, some of us believe that we should give adequate attention at this consultation to material sharing and economic issues, and I hope that we would be able to deal with that, though it may not be a very pleasant task. The material sharing is a spiritual exercise, and we should look at the issue in its totality and in a holistic way. Sharing was going on in the church long before ecumenical organizations came into being. My own experiences are limited to the last 15 years when I got involved in monitoring resources for efforts for the total transformation of society in Asia. It has not been easy, as anyone would agree. But now we have come to a point in history where we can take stock of our positions, priorities, relationships in a mature way, in an atmosphere of growing mutual trust and openness. I am happy to say that in my understanding there has been a lot of progress during these years in this respect. I would like to identify the following areas:

1. Moving towards a common perspective. There is a growing awareness that we all live and operate under sinful structures and systems. We
are a broken human community riddled with exploitation, oppression,
marginalization. However, a search is on for an authentic human community. In churches and institutions in the North some have shown that they
want to be part of this search which affirms mutuality and solidarity.

2. Participation in decision-making. This is a tricky issue, and we have
a long way to go. The Asia Forum organized by ICCO with CCA made
some headway and pointed to possibilities such as internationalization of
decision-making. However, this area is still a difficult one and much
more remains to be done.

In the ecumenical fellowship, the Asia regional group has made much
progress. This group has evolved into a representative body able to deal
with issues and concerns. However, only a small portion of the flow of
money from North to South is involved in this.

As long as the donor-recipient relationship is maintained, one wonders
how any meaningful and creative participation in decision-making will be
possible.

3. Growing sharing within the region. Sharing of personnel and
material resources does take place within Asian countries, though in a
limited way. Hong Kong, Korea, Japan, Taiwan — of course Aotearoa/
New Zealand and Australia are taking the lead in this respect. There is a
growing Asian solidarity and support of each other not only in material
terms, but also by expressing solidarity particularly in times of crisis.
Two weeks ago I was in Japan for a church leaders meeting. During a
reception by the NCC Japan, a Japanese woman who had lived in
Singapore with her husband and had returned to Japan when her husband
died at the age of 43, made a substantial contribution to CCA's human
rights programme. It is not the amount of money that is important, but the
intention of these Japanese friends to participate in the struggle for human
rights and dignity in Asia; and this act brought tears to the eyes of all
those who were present.

4. Education for resource-sharing. It is still a fact that many donor
agencies insist on stories and images of suffering to raise their funds.
But some of them try to use at least part of their money for meaningful
development and human rights work. In Asia there have been various
efforts to help agencies in a proper understanding of what is at stake.

I am grateful for this occasion to share these insights and experiences.
A number of people from both the South and North at this conference are
somewhat cynical as to its chances to achieve much. I myself occasion-

ally feel that way. But I believe if we can be open and bold enough to break new ground, we can go a long way in growing together.

George Ninan

Uruguay and Central America: sharing in suffering and struggle

Uruguay, like many other Latin American countries, suffered from a dictatorial regime for almost twelve years. It was a time of anguish and suffering for the people. The state of law had gone, torture and prison were daily realities. Today, with the return of democracy, there are still many wounds. One of these is the fear that a similar situation may occur again. In this context the church feels the need to be with the people. One of the concrete ways in which it has been trying to do so is the exchange of young people with churches in various countries. This has helped the church in Uruguay to realize that there are brothers and sisters in other parts of the world who want to be in solidarity. It has helped these young people to discover the situation of a poor country and to understand the inter-relationship between rich and poor nations.

Diaconia is an ecumenical organization of the Lutheran, Baptist and Roman Catholic churches in *El Salvador* which is involved in humanitarian work. When it was about to be closed down by the repressive forces, the WCC organized an ecumenical team visit to the country, composed of brothers and sisters from different parts of the world. This made it possible to stop the repression, but above all it was a concrete experience of pastoral care for the churches and the people of El Salvador in their suffering and their quest for justice. It is an illustration of international solidarity in the defence of life so threatened and so easily destroyed in this part of the world. At this moment Bishop Medardo Gómez of the Lutheran Church is under threat of death; already there has been a bomb placed in the premises of his church. There has been a lot of solidarity on the part of many churches to see that this threat does not become a reality. Intercession is also called for. Certainly, there will be martyrs, but our desire is that our brothers and sisters and the people of Latin America may live.

As coordinator of the Latin American group for ecumenical sharing I have visited some projects in Central America. Of the experiences that I have had the most valuable is the sharing of life itself, the sharing of the struggles for justice, the sharing of the hope that the kingdom of God may become a reality. In these experiences financial aid is only an element that makes it possible to respond immediately to the problems of survival of women, youth and children in this region. In the sharing in these situations the churches are working together with the social and popular organizations because they believe that it is God's people who are on the road to liberation.

Mario Dabalá

Youth: two questions to the churches

Youth are the grassroots. We are the grassroots of the church and society. We are not satisfied with the way we have been invited to participate in this resource-sharing consultation.

The process for this consultation has been going on for years, yet youth have not been included in this process as they should have been. Consequently, we did not have adequate time to state our problems and specific concerns in our various regions. We will continue to reflect on these concerns and struggles throughout this conference in the regional and working groups.

Our primary concern now is the ecumenical sharing of young people in the ecumenical sharing of resources.

Young people around the world are bearing the heavy burden of the world's pain and injustice. Churches need to know and hear the experiences of young people.

Young people need solidarity, resources and support through the ecumenical movement.

Youth organizations, networks and projects need the support and the trust of those who have themselves once been young.

Youth are the church today as well as tomorrow and are demanding to be accepted as full members in the decision-making and action in the churches' work for truth, justice and peace.

In this context we demand that you bring these questions to your work in this conference and to your churches.

We have many gifts and resources to share. Are you, as churches, willing to receive and share them? For example:

1. Are you seeking the experience and opinions of young people in your decisions and working processes in the ecumenical sharing of resources?

2. Are you fully supporting the struggles, work and organizations of young people committed to ecumenical visions at all levels — local, national, regional and international?

Women: as far as we are concerned... the question of justice

We have had little time and been under pressure to prepare our input into the draft document. But we do have common concerns as women who relate to this discussion on ecumenical sharing, and we want to name them. Our specific proposals will come later.

The first thing we want to say is that all of our concerns have to do with the question of justice, the very core of what we are as a human family and who we are specifically as children of God. You know our stories — we have told them time and time again. The time of hearing yet another set of stories in this kind of meeting is past. Our patience is wearing thin at pleading to be included, to be "allowed" to participate, as if one part of this body would have the right to "allow" while the other parts have to beg for their rights. Tokenism in terms of participation, in terms of sharing what we have, is no longer sufficient.

Sithembiso Nyoni in her presentation underlined that "resource-sharing without national and international political action to correct the situation of need ends up creating long-term negative effects". So our overarching concern is that the document coming out of this consultation does not deal in the first instance with how to make the "project system" better — although we do need to address that — but with the restructuring of the global economy, with issues like the international debt crisis, trade patterns, aid policies, human rights violations, etc. As far as we women are concerned, effective sharing of material resources can only happen if these broader issues are addressed, and if those who share (both sides) commit themselves to acting politically.

Follow-up

Letter from the General Secretary

To all member churches and members of Central Committee,
associate councils and regional ecumenical bodies,
related agencies for mission, service and development

Dear friends,

On 24-31 October 1987 the world consultation on resource sharing took place in El Escorial, Spain, under the theme "Koinonia — Sharing Life in a World Community". At the end of an intensive week of shared worship life, Bible study, discussions in working groups and regional meetings, the delegates committed themselves to an ecumenical discipline of "Guidelines for Sharing". The enclosed text which was adopted unanimously by the participants sets out strongly and unequivocally their common convictions: the theological basis, the "rules" for sharing in 13 points and some consequences for implementation, as well as the commitment.

By adopting this discipline for sharing, the consultation achieved its main goal of bringing to fruition more than ten years of study and reflection on the ecumenical sharing of resources. It puts the result before the WCC, the churches and their agencies, not in the usual form of recommendations, but first and foremost as a *call to commitment:* a call to subscribe to this discipline and to put it into practice.

I should like to underline and bring to your attention the importance of the discipline which has emerged from the El Escorial meeting and its call to commitment. I am asking you therefore to consider how your church, your council or agency could begin the process of receiving these "Guidelines for Sharing" and responding to the commitment. Do you confirm the basic affirmation of this discipline? Do you commit yourself — as a church, a council, an agency — to abide by it in all your national and international sharing relations? Do you encourage the WCC and the ecumenical family to apply this discipline in all our reciprocal relations? We hope that a thorough discussion will now take place in the churches, councils, in their agencies for mission, diaconal service and development where these exist, with a view towards action on the proposed discipline. This should take into account the long-term implications for our policies and structures of sharing.

The participants have pledged to give an account of their commitment within a period of three years. The full report of the consultation will be published in the coming months. The Executive Committee in March and the Central Committee in August will discuss the report and give guidance for action, both with regard to the WCC itself and to the member churches. The WCC Seventh Assembly in Canberra, three years from now, might well offer the opportunity to report on the actions of the churches, and to consider future common action.

Further details of this process, in which I am urging all our member churches and affiliated councils to join, will follow in due course. El Escorial has brought before us a challenge for renewal in a vital area of the ecumenical movement. Those who were there have witnessed a deep sense of community and common purpose — with gratitude they say that the Spirit moved. Let us be ready to hear and to act.

Yours in Christ,

EMILIO CASTRO
General Secretary   January 1988

Excerpt from the Minutes of the Central Committe of the WCC, August 1988

The Committee received with gratitude the report on the world consultation on resource-sharing. It welcomed the "El Escorial Guidelines for Sharing" as the fruit of the study programme on ecumenical sharing of resources. The Committee noted with satisfaction the support of the programme units for this new discipline. The Committee considered the proposals for implementation of the "Guidelines for Sharing", with regard to the WCC and the member churches. It recognized that the recommendations on women and youth adopted by the world consultation are intended to further the participation of women and youth as stated in the "Guidelines", in the area of ecumenical sharing of resources.

Recommendations

Taking into account the comments received from the programme units, the Committee recommends that the Central Committee:

1) receive the "Guidelines for Sharing" *and recommendations on women and youth* formulated at the world consultation on resource-sharing;

2) affirm the WCC's commitment to the discipline emerging from the "Guidelines" *and recommendations on women and youth,* and instruct the commissions and working groups to work out the implications for their sub-unit, with regard to their programme activities and their sharing instruments;

3) call the member churches to receive the "Guidelines for Sharing" *and the recommendations on women and youth,* to respond to the commitment, and to implement the discipline in their own situation.

The Central Committee accepted these recommendations, and in addition

4) requested the general secretary to report to each meeting of the Central Committee on progress made in implementation of the "Guidelines for Sharing" of resources.

Response to the commitment: some suggestions for follow-up action

— Make the theme of "sharing life" central to worship and celebration. It can be integrated into the liturgy in many different ways. Use the worship book of the world consultation as a resource. Celebrate the commitment to share life with other churches or groups nearby and from abroad. Invite women, young people, marginalized groups, to bring their experience. "Sharing life" fits very well with celebrations centred on justice, peace and the integrity of creation.

— Use the "Guidelines for Sharing" and all the material of this report as an ecumenical resource for reflection in your church or organization on the issues of sharing resources, for education programmes, communication, etc.

— Identify those points in the "Guidelines for Sharing" and the recommendations on women and youth which are of particular relevance for your church or organization. Work out proposals around these points. Develop a time-frame and set goals for a process of decision-making and implementation of the proposals.

Example: The Swiss delegates adopted this method on their return from the world consultation. Less than a year later the Federation of Protestant Churches of Switzerland had taken its first decision, on 50% women and 20% youth, to be implemented within three years.
— Ask the appropriate body (or several) in the church to study the "Guidelines for Sharing" and the recommendations and to prepare a proposal for reception and response, with recommendations for implementation, to the governing body (e.g. the synod, general assembly, convention, board, as applicable).
Example: The United Church of Canada did so. Its Division of World Outreach prepared a resolution for the synod which adopted the "Guidelines" as a policy document for the Division. NB: To help the church understand the "Guidelines" better, the DWO turned each one of them into questions related to their own situation.
— Make use of the "Guidelines for Sharing" in particular relations of partnership of your church or organization with other churches or related bodies. Consider whether the "Guidelines" could become the basis of existing or new partnerships. Make growing towards a "covenant-relationship for sharing life" the goal. Use the "Guidelines" to test relationships and as a tool to solve conflicts.
— Organize an exercise of mutual accountability, e.g. by inviting an ecumenical team to visit your church or organization and to examine with you your priorities, procedures for decision-making, structures, etc. Draw conclusions and plan together for action. Enable such a visiting team to meet the "grassroots".
— Form a group of individual persons who are committed to the "Guidelines for Sharing". Identify together the possibilities for action and map out strategies.
— Contextualize the "Guidelines for Sharing" by "translating" them into the situation of the church, the country, the region... Develop your own commitment to a "covenant of sharing life in a world community".

You could adopt one suggested action or several at a time — it all depends on the situation. Plan towards the Seventh Assembly of the WCC in 1991 for an expression of commitment to the ecumenical discipline. Make use of the WCC secretariat for ecumenical sharing, which is responsible for follow-up: send information on what you are doing; ask for information on what is being done elsewhere; ask for material, ideas, visits.

The Story of ESR

When in 1977 the consultation on "Conditions for Sharing" was held in Glion as the first major step in the study on ecumenical sharing of resources there were probably few participants who would have expected that the theme would become so central to the life of the WCC in the ensuing period. Ten years later this centrality was vividly expressed in the event that took place at El Escorial and its theme "Koinonia — Sharing Life in a World Community", not only as the culmination of a long process but also because this was one of the five Council-wide world meetings on the way to the Seventh Assembly in 1991.

A study, a system, a discipline

The process of reflection on ESR has gone through several stages. It began as a study programme called for by the Central Committee in 1976, following the Nairobi Assembly where interchurch aid, mission and development had been discussed in the wake of the debate on moratorium. The call for a moratorium on the sending of personnel and funds, launched by some church leaders in Asia and Africa in the early seventies, had raised fundamental questions about the selfhood of the "receiving" churches and the self-understanding of churches accustomed to seeing themselves solely as senders and givers. The ESR study was undertaken as an effort to provide an ecumenical platform for reflection. It was entrusted to the Commission on Inter-Church Aid, Refugee and World Service (CICARWS), in close relationship with the Commission on World Mission and Evangelism (CWME).

In 1980 a report was brought to the Central Committee, which issued a "Message to the Churches", commended the study guide *Empty Hands* for use by the churches and directed all three programme units of the WCC to reflect together on the implications of the ESR study. Two specific issues were lifted up in the report, i.e. the sharing of people and the question of government funding. In the following period the effort to implement ESR concentrated on the elaboration of a new "resource-sharing system". The idea was to apply such principles as mutuality, transparency and joint decision-making in the first place to the various sharing instruments of the WCC itself and to enhance the participation of the churches and agencies in the ecumenical system. A highlight of this period was the consultation held at Glion in February 1982, co-sponsored by CICARWS, CWME and the Commission on the Churches' Participation in Development (CCPD). The other sub-units concerned with sharing resources also became involved and ESR or "resource-sharing" became a Council-wide issue. A staff task force on resource-sharing was set up; the first WCC Resource Sharing Book was published in 1982 and by 1983 the regional resource-sharing groups were formed. The desk responsible for ESR was moved from CICARWS to the General Secretariat. This search for a system was not without tensions within (and outside) the WCC because it created an impression of centralization.

At the Vancouver Assembly (1983) ESR was discussed in Issue Group 4, "Healing and Sharing Life in Community". The Assembly put the implementation of the resource-sharing system under the priority areas of the WCC, in terms of the "comprehensive understanding of ESR and as part of a continuing dialogue on the mission and service of the church... to facilitate models of ecumenical sharing and not to create a heavy, centralized structure". This meant that a new, more flexible approach was necessary. It led to a third stage, in which the focus was the ecumenical commitment to the sharing of resources and hence the need to work out a common basis or, as it was called, an ecumenical discipline as a guide for new relationships of sharing. Implied in it was the recognition of a shift in the WCC's primary vocation from administrating a project system to promoting the commitment to an ecumenical vision. Much clarification was still needed, but ESR had embarked on a course that proved to be worthwhile.

A widening circle

The participants in the first period of reflection on ESR were mainly the agencies, churches and national councils related to the interchurch aid project system. At a later stage, especially after the Vancouver Assembly, the circle became much wider with the involvement of the mission agencies, the regional ecumenical bodies, the network groups of CCPD, Urban Rural Mission (URM), the Programme to Combat Racism (PCR),

Women, Youth, etc. Slowly the churches in the North have also begun to see the relevance of ESR for their own life and witness.

Obstacles encountered

The ESR process has never been easy. One of the greatest obstacles has been — and continues to be — the difficulty to translate the concept into structural changes in the existing relationships of giving and receiving. Related to this is the tension between the search for practical solutions on the one hand and the attention given to fundamental questions of theology, socio-economic issues, the specific regional situations, etc. on the other hand. Often the priorities of the participants are divided along these very lines! Another problem lies in the distinction between "material" and "non-material" resources and the difficulty to include both in a comprehensive approach to sharing. Spiritual values do not lend themselves to the type of transfer as a project grant. A third question which has been at the heart of the ESR debate is that of the bilateral relationships versus the ecumenical channels which are mutilateral in nature. The great diversity of the participants in the process and of the regions has also contributed to its complexity. No wonder there was and is sometimes frustration about the seeming lack of tangible changes. The sort of transformation a concept like ESR calls for is so radical that it either happens slowly — as is in fact the case when one looks back over a sufficiently long period of time — or comes in ways which are unexpected.

Sharing of people

In the history of the WCC, ESR had a forerunner called Ecumenical Sharing of Personnel (ESP). When the Central Committee received the report on the study in 1980 it recommended that renewed attention be given to the sharing of human resources. This became a programmatic activity of CICARWS, which initiated many innovative experiences of exchange of people. The reflection on ESR was often challenged and enriched by these concrete illustrations of sharing; it has been said again and again that the greatest resource of the church is the people, and that ecumenical sharing must always be people-centred.

Use of government funds

Another issue which was identified especially in the context of the project system was the role of financial resources made available by some governments of the industrialized countries for church-related development projects. A consultation was called together in 1983 for an ecumenical discussion on this subject. In the period September 1985 to December 1986 a survey was carried out, the findings of which were published in the report *The Development Market*. This question of government funding has gradually become a concern for ongoing ecumenical reflection and consultation, within the framework of ESR.

The world consultation

In 1985 the Central Committee agreed with the proposal for a world consultation on resource-sharing to be held in October 1987. A planning group of ten persons was appointed by the Executive Committee to prepare the consultation in cooperation with the staff task force. The planning group met three times, in January and September 1986 and in February 1987. At its second meeting the group prepared a paper on the purpose of the world consultation, stating the aim "to agree on an ecumenical discipline for the sharing of resources and to foster a process of commitment to such a discipline". This was approved by the Executive Committee in September 1986. The planning group took responsibility for all the major aspects of the consultation: working document, participants, programme, theme, etc. This world consultation was one of the rare events within the life of the WCC which took place outside the sponsorship of any particular programme unit or sub-unit.

Theme

In choosing the theme "Koinonia — Sharing Life in a World Community", the planning group declared its hope that sharing would be understood not just in terms of resources but of "sharing life", with all God's people who together form the community of the world. This is indeed the vision of the "Guidelines": a covenant for sharing life. The theme was also intended to signify the relation with the other council-wide events, i.e. "Diakonia 2000 — Called to be Neighbours", "Your Will Be Done: Mission in Christ's Way" and "Justice, Peace and Integrity of Creation," on the way to the Seventh Assembly.

Working document

At an early stage of the planning for the world consultation it had been suggested that a "working document" be prepared proposing elements of the ecumenical discipline. Such a document would make it possible to benefit fully from the insights gained in the ESR process and to help the conference not to start the discussion all over again. As it happened, the working document also enabled a more participatory preparation. A first draft was published and widely circulated in March 1987. Many comments were received and incorporated into a revised version, the draft working document, which was sent to the participants before they came to the conference.

Regional perspectives

The regional pre-consultations were another important aspect of the preparation. Five of these took place in March-April 1987, in the form of enlarged meetings of the regional resource sharing groups in Africa, Asia, Latin America, Middle East and Pacific. They were followed by two more, in Europe and the Caribbean, in a slightly different setting. Unfortunately it was not possible to organize a similar meeting in North America. The reports of these regional pre-consultations were shared with all the participants and constituted an important input to the world consultation. The earlier ones were also extensively used for the revision of the working document, which had been discussed in the March-April series of meetings.

A real meeting

In the planning, the world consultation itself was mainly conceived as a working conference, centred on the draft working document. The programme was planned in three stages: input through plenary presentations, Bible study and testimonies; a first round of working groups on sections of the draft working document; reporting followed by a second round of working groups and adoption of a final document. The rationale for this process and its purpose were shared with the participants right from the beginning. As the working groups went about their task two things began to emerge: a sense that the conference could and should do more than review a carefully prepared document, and the urgency, for the participants from the South, to discuss the issues in their own regional setting. Admittedly there was hesitation to change the process among those who were responsible for it, but eventually room was made for the conference to take its own course. Had this not been done, the meeting would have been a failure. The strongly expressed need to work in regional groupings towards the common result (i.e. the "Guidelines") was probably significant for the ecumenical movement today as a whole. Working groups which reflect all our diversity of culture, region, confession, gender and age may not always be the best model for struggling with our divisions! Yet the changes which occurred did not mean a rejection of the work done in the first round of the programme. In the final plenary it was agreed that the findings of the working groups should be compiled to become the "longer" part of the conference report (in contrast to the "Guidelines" referred to as the "shorter" part). Another piece of work which could not be finished at the meeting and was therefore left for follow-up, was to supplement the "Guidelines" with biblical passages, stories, commentaries, etc. The final plenary was marked by a genuine concern that the commitments taken be also implemented; there was a proposal to appoint to this effect a group made up of conference participants. After an intensive debate the decision was taken to ask the WCC to take responsibility for the follow-up.

Worship

The obvious impact of the worship life of the conference was largely due to the careful preparatory work that went into it. Except for the closing service all the liturgies were composed beforehand and put together in a special worship book. All through the meeting, a team of gifted persons from different regions gathered each day with the celebrants to rehearse the service of the following day, the music, etc. Several symbolic acts reflecting the cultural diversity of the participants were built into the services. The hymns that were sung and the music came from many regions and traditions. The sense of community was sustained by the real participation of all.

Facts and figures

When for reasons of cost it was decided to hold the world consultation in Europe the planning group expressed its preference for a place that would not carry a "donor" image. El Escorial, a small town 40 kms southwest of Madrid, fulfilled this criterion; on the other hand, this venue, once a stronghold of ecclesiastical and colonial imperialism, also had a symbolic meaning which was highlighted several times. The meeting took place on the premises of Residencia San José, a Roman Catholic conference centre whose simple but adequate facilities were consonant with the conference theme. It was the first time that the Spanish member churches of the WCC hosted an ecumenical gathering of this size. Their assistance with local organization, the visits to congregations in Madrid, the opportunity to learn about the history and witness of the Reformation in Spain, the encounters with the leaders of these churches and also with representatives of the Roman Catholic Church — they were enriching experiences for all.

There were 229 participants at El Escorial: 122 delegates representing churches, councils and agencies, 49 delegates representing sub-unit networks and related organizations, 12 fraternal delegates, 9 resource persons, 17 observers representing international organizations (including 4 from the Roman Catholic Church) and 20 programme staff. Of these 229 participants 74 were women and 21 youth; 46 technical, support and coopted staff and 22 stewards helped with the organization of the meetings; 9 persons participated as visitors.

The very mode of invitation for the consultation, i.e. asking churches, etc. to appoint their delegate(s), had given rise to serious questioning as to whether there would be adequate participation of women. Eventually the 30% target was achieved, but the role the women participants played in the consultation went far beyond their numerical strength. They assumed 50% of the tasks of group leaders, recorders, drafters, celebrants, etc. and met frequently as a group in between sessions.

A special effort had also been made to reach the target of 15% youth. Unfortunately this failed, for several reasons: it happened too late and several young people either did not answer in time or declined at the last moment. Some others, on the contrary, did come in spite of very short notice, but found themselves unprepared. The young people took part very actively in the meeting, but it was frustrating for the group as a whole not to be able to make its presence more felt.

Towards the Assembly
The participants at El Escorial committed themselves to give an account to each other, and so to God, of the ways in which they have turned their words into deeds, within a period of three years. That is, towards the end of 1990. The Central Committee, in receiving the "Guidelines" and recommendations, affirming the WCC's commitment and asking the churches to do likewise, at its August 1988 meeting also responded to the call of the conference that the WCC take charge of follow-up. A new mandate of the secretariat for ESR was approved to that effect, for the period up and through the Seventh Assembly. It includes both action within the WCC and with the member churches. *Rendez-vous* has been taken to give account of what has been done, and to work towards an act of commitment by the churches as they gather together at the Assembly in February 1991.

Enlarged Meetings of the Regional Resource-Sharing Groups 1987

Introduction

In preparation for the world consultation on resource-sharing held 24-31 October, 1987, in El Escorial, Spain, an international effort was made to seek regional input through a process of regional reflection on resource sharing. Between 25 March and 29 April 1987, five consultations in Africa, Asia, Latin America, the Middle East, and the Pacific were organized primarily in the form of enlarged annual meetings of the regional resource-sharing groups. In September, two other pre-consultation meetings were held in Europe and the Caribbean. The purpose of each of these meetings was to provide the opportunity for regional consideration of ecumenical resource-sharing, particularly in preparation for the world consultation on resource-sharing, and in light of the world consultation on inter-church aid, refugee and world service (Larnaca, 1986). The full reports of these pre-consultations constituted one portion of the preparatory material for El Escorial, thereby emphasizing the importance of regional analyses and relationships within the resource-sharing process.

Each regional meeting provided valuable insight into the nature and specifics of resource-sharing. Together, these regional meetings emphasized certain issues which were to form and inform the work of the world consultation:

a) the urgency of radical changes in the prevailing donor-recipient relationships;
b) the movement towards sharing and solidarity between churches and communities in the South;
c) the affirmation of commitment to share ecumenically;
d) the vision of a church that shares because it is committed to the people, especially the poor;

e) the emphasis on decision-making at the local/national or sub-regional level.

The reports which follow summarize the discussion and recommendations of these very important regional meetings.

AFRICA

The enlarged meeting of the Africa resource sharing group was held 25-27 March 1987 in Arusha, Tanzania. Introductory presentations provided the background and described the purposes of the consultation. Mr Toko Gumedzoe from Togo spoke about the values of sharing in African culture and tradition. Rev. Clement Janda, general secretary of the Sudan Christian Council, spoke about the involvement of the African churches in mission and development, and their overseas relationships. On the basis of this input, five issues were identified for small group consideration. All groups were asked to deal with the question of participation of women and youth.

Group 1: Values of sharing from the African tradition

This group explored the implications of the traditional African values of loving and sharing, for the process of resource-sharing. Two aspects of these traditional values were emphasized. The first is that the very rich traditional African manner of sharing includes visible as well as invisible resources. Secondly, these values of sharing are marked by a mutuality of give and take, where clear expectations exist that the one in need will articulate the need and so make the need clear within the whole community. It was felt that while the specifics of African sharing have changed because of urbanization and the monetarization of the economy, the spirit of sharing is still alive.

The group emphasized that the traditional values of African sharing have much to offer to the international process of resource-sharing. Too often the visible and invisible gifts of the South are excluded from a one-way sharing process. It was felt that the commonly practised tradition of sharing skills gratuitously within the community could be applied in ecumenical communities at all levels. As well, the traditional African experience of community unity within which sharing was practised, and which was disrupted when missionaries introduced denominational divisions into traditional African social patterns, could be revived within ecumenical sharing. To further strengthen this unity, the groups emphasized the need to develop sharing of visible and invisible resources locally, nationally and regionally in addition to the need to improve the already existing North-South system.

Group 2: Towards a new system of sharing

This group stressed that the current well-established resource-sharing patterns, both bilateral and ecumenical, do not allow for true sharing, and therefore have failed both the North and the South. The nature of these patterns are related to the history of the colonial economic relationships between the North and the South, a history which has been duplicated in the mission patterns of the churches. At the present time, churches in both the North and South operate within a system of economic oppression of the South by the North, and this makes it necessary to raise certain questions concerning the socio-political environment of the churches. For exploitative relationships to change, it is necessary that the churches in the North change the present stance of their governments.

Because of the immensity and complexity of resource-sharing problems, it is necessary for the church to develop a clear vision of the future it wants, and to be prepared to initiate a radical change within itself and in society at large. The church must stand willing to be a church: (1) which practises holistic theology; (2) which through prophetic example is committed to eliminating all forces, structures and systems of injustice in society; (3) which cherishes and works for self-reliance, including economic self-reliance; (4) which is committed to responsible resource management and renewal economically as well as environmentally; (5) which is committed to serving and working with all God's people, including mobilizing them for relevant action.

The vision of the future includes an understanding of ecumenical sharing in which there are no more donor-recipient institutions, but rather an emphasis on mutual interdependency. It also includes a commitment to acquiring information and training which will bring about change. For African churches, this includes a preparedness to move away from dependency relationships, to define more clearly the conditions for receiving external aid, and to strengthen mechanisms to increase South-South relationships as well as local leadership training and infrastructure.

Group 3: Relevant education for sharing, solidarity and justice

This group placed its discussion of relevant education within the context of traditional African education which offered to all people education that was relative to the community. This was contrasted with

the current colonial system of education, including theological education, which is marked by limited access, and the content of which is
relevant only to producing functionaries for the system. The task which
lies ahead is to change the system to facilitate education that fosters
sharing, solidarity and justice at the community level; which prepares
people for life; which makes people conscious of the environment in
which they live; which makes people whole; and which liberates the
people.

Such relevant education would have identifiable characteristics. Education should provide animators and community leaders, empower people
to become change-makers, and facilitate the initiatives of grassroots
people to liberate themselves. Relevant education must include informal
education through workshops, seminars, etc. for the purpose of training
and leadership formation. For all aspects of relevant education, questions
must be asked to determine who sets the educational agenda, who
controls content, etc.

Ten models of education were identified as appropriate for relevant
education: (1) training for leadership of people not connected with
institutions; (2) community organization to empower people as change-
makers; (3) conscientization to make people critically conscious of the
oppressive structures and ideologies around them; (4) education with
production, to allow students to gain knowledge and also control the
means of production; (5) decentralization, including the transfer of
power and decision-making to the communities (not a transfer of power
to local manifestations of institutions); (6) theological education by
extension with attention given to contextualizing content to make it
relevant to the needs and aspirations of the communities in which those
trained are to work; (7) education for resistance to invasion and control,
keeping in mind that poverty makes it difficult for people to be engaged
in sustained resistance; (8) networking, as a way of creating linkages
among people's movements to foster solidarity and sharing; (9) prog-
ramming and training skills, including literature production; (10) training institutions as places of creative reflection even for communities at
the grassroots level.

Group 4: Political issues
This group discussed the elimination of root causes of poverty, hunger
and powerlessness; the redistribution of wealth; new methods of evangelization in Africa; and participation by women and youth in resource-
sharing.

The problems of African dependency were discussed in relation to the fact that Africa was once self-sufficient. In the light of the situation in Africa, Christians have a special responsibility to become involved in the service of the powerless, work together for change, put pressure on governments, and reveal what is really happening in economic institutions.

The churches in Africa also face a challenge in evangelization presented by well-financed and media-wise fundamentalists from North America and Europe who are seen to undermine the stability of African churches, use religion to draw people away from social issues, focus on the hereafter to divert attention from the political situation, and abuse religion to attain certain ideological ends. African churches must examine their own understanding of evangelism to determine whether biblical teaching is sufficient to allow people to identify abuse of their faith, and whether it is possible to be better witnesses, practising what is preached.

It was *recommended* that the El Escorial meeting should be postponed if participation of women and youth according to the World Council of Churches quotas could not be guaranteed. These quotas should also determine project decisions, and churches should be challenged to indicate where they stand or how they have implemented the quotas.

Group 5: Theological issues

This group addressed the question of how to redistribute the wealth God has given. The biblical witness that God has created a world rich in human, material and spiritual resources of which people are only stewards was affirmed, and biblical examples of sharing were discussed.

Four hindrances to resource-sharing were identified: the sin of selfishness; the belief that money is power; the use of aid as a political weapon; the mistaken tendency of people in the South to think that they have nothing to share.

Sharing can be strengthened by actions taken to educate ourselves about stewardship, the justice of sharing, and by changing attitudes concerning the rich resources that the South has to offer. It is important to maintain an emphasis on the sharing of spiritual as well as material resources. Christians in Africa have a lot to contribute in spiritual resources which are tapped from African traditional values, the Bible, and from the life of the African church.

It is important to foster closer ties with the independent churches. There is much to be learned from their evangelistic methods. These ties could be developed through dialogue, ecumenical and interfaith services, theological exchanges, pulpit exchanges, joint development projects, and invitations for participation by national Christian councils.

Barriers to women and youth were identified in African culture as well as in the church, although the biblical equality of women and men was affirmed. Equal opportunity rather than balance of sexes at meetings was regarded as important, although it was stated that women should be given every opportunity to acquire appropriate abilities and qualifications. The role of husband and wife in the home should be redefined in such a way that natural roles are not violated; and at the same time inhumane aspects in those roles should be eradicated. Youth should be trained and encouraged to participate fully in the decision-making in the church.

Recommendations
1. African churches and councils should set aside resources (human, material, financial) to help sister churches in Africa in times of crisis. Some emergency funds, however minimal, should be included in the regular budgets of the churches for this purpose.
2. The traditional African values of sharing should be lifted up and put at the service of ecumenical resource-sharing.
3. The churches should be conscientized about their rich spiritual resources and churches in the South should share the abundance of their spiritual resources with the churches in the North.
4. Programmes of resource-sharing among the churches in the South should be promoted.
5. The African churches must commit themselves to serving and working with all God's people, in a holistic way.
6. Steps should be taken to foster mutual relationships and understanding between mainline churches and the independent/indigenous churches.
7. The church leaders must show active commitment and solidarity in the struggle for justice, peace and the integrity of creation.
8. Existing networks should be strengthened and new ones established to provide analysis of the root causes of suffering, and these studies should be widely publicized together with real life stories about exploitation and human suffering.
9. Church structures at the local level must be empowered for decision-making and priority-setting.
10. External funding should be made use of to facilitate implementation of projects and programmes and not used to exercise power.

11. The churches should commit themselves to eliminating existing structures which do not encourage mutual sharing in the local situation.
12. The African churches should re-examine the content and methods of their theological training, especially for the lay people, in order to build educational programmes that encourage sharing, solidarity, justice, selfhood and participation.
13. In view of the fact that 99.5% of church membership are lay, the African churches should devote much more of their resources (financial and human) to implementing the above-mentioned programmes. Special attention should be given to improving the skills of trainers.
14. Relevant training should emphasize development of community-oriented skills. The ecumenical media network should be encouraged to promote new models through information-sharing. Exchange through inter-community visits is strongly recommended.
15. The ecumenical family should identify, encourage and facilitate grassroots initiatives especially in innovating and developing new approaches to education and training.
16. The spirit of the Jubilee Year should be revived, and appropriate models of ecumenical sharing devised and implemented.
17. Women and youth must participate fully in the decision-making of the church.
18. The Office for Resource Sharing should adhere to the WCC rules for the participation of women and youth in the world consultation on resource-sharing, or else postpone the consultation until these rules have been met.

ASIA

The Asia resource sharing group was organized jointly by the Christian Conference of Asia (CCA) and the World Council of Churches in Singapore, 29-31 March 1987. Opening discussions included presentations on the Asian perspective of resource-sharing by Dr Feliciano Carino and Rev. Pritram Santram. Four issue areas were identified for work by three small groups: (1) theological perspective; (2) mechanisms for resource-sharing, (3) models of sharing, and (4) commitment to resource-sharing and the poor.

Group 1: Theological perspective/commitment to resource-sharing and the poor

The task of this group was to explore the theological aspects of the nature of the commitment to resource-sharing, and to identify the best pattern of relationships for attaining solidarity, justice and participation in struggle.

The theological discussion centred on the ambiguities and limitations inherent in the use of specific symbols or paradigms in the discussion of resource-sharing. The image of the eucharist, for example, was seen to be problematic because of its exclusivity as a liturgical symbol, particularly in Asia's multi-religious context. At the same time, the possibilities of the eucharist as symbol were noted in that a retrieval of its original status and application offers a revolutionary significance in the life of the people and the church today. In the eucharist a community comes together to form a just society and offer a true reflection of the body broken for the world. Although other paradigms were identified (the eschatological meal, the new creation) it was agreed that all paradigms are inadequate and limited for containing the dimensions necessary in the process of sharing.

The discussion of the nature of commitment to resource-sharing affirmed that the theological basis of commitment should be closely scrutinized. Commitment begins where the people are, and it involves elements of obedience. Discussion pointed to the different levels of commitment, and the recognition that sharing involves conscientizing and raising levels of commitment, as well as conversion and transformation of individuals. Sharing of resources is difficult in situations where, although a high level of trust exists, a fundamental disagreement of vision makes true sharing impossible. It is important that our commitment to solidarity with justice for, and sharing with, the poor and especially those engaged in struggle is conveyed to those who do not share this vision, or who are at a different level of commitment. This may involve serious dialogue, or even conflict, so that some form of working reconciliation is possible for the goal of sharing. If there is not some sharing of vision, then sharing of resources compromises the integrity of concerned parties. If there is not some mutuality of trust then any common work becomes impossible to achieve. Thus, there should be some real dialogue for setting up priorities and visions between donor agencies as well as receiving groups.

Patterns of sharing should break out of classical church-to-church sharing and include church-to-people and people-to-people sharing. Varied patterns of sharing also allow for flexibility for sharing within politically sensitive situations.

Group 2: Mechanisms for ecumenical sharing of resources

This group recommended that participatory ecumenical mechanisms be devised at the national, regional and international levels through which both donor and receiver partners in resource-sharing could engage in listening to each other and responding ecumenically to need in a context of mutual accountability and transparency. Four levels of sharing mechanisms were recommended, with the understanding that altogether new ecumenical structures were not implied in addition to existing national, regional and international structures.

a) *National level:* A national ecumenical body would be composed of representatives of churches and appropriate service/programme agencies including representatives of action groups to: (1) determine ecumenical priorities at the national level and to develop ecumenical commitment to these priorities; (2) be responsible for mutual transparency and accountability among all partners; (3) evaluate and review priorities and processes; (4) share information about programme, priorities and ecumenical or other bilateral or multilateral relationships.

b) *National level with international participation:* A body would be set up for the purpose of helping the donor agencies to appreciate national needs and the priorities of receiving churches and action groups, and to challenge them to commitment, so promoting ecumenical relationships and mutual understanding. It would also provide the opportunity for the national body to raise questions about the priorities and modes of operation of the external partners.

c) *Regional level:* An ecumenical body similar to a regional council or conference of churches (e.g. CCA) would monitor and organize programmes of exchange of personnel and of ecumenical sharing of non-material resources, as well as of human resource development, and to act as a liaison between the national ecumenical bodies and the international ecumenical body for interpreting the needs, priorities, mandates and resources of the one to the other.

d) *International (global) level:* An international ecumenical body like the WCC would bring together representatives of various partner churches and agencies to: (1) share information about the priorities, mandates, modes of operation and relationships of these bodies; (2) develop a system of mutual transparency and accountability among these bodies and the churches to which they relate; and (3) to question and revise, when possible, the priorities and modes of operation of these bodies and to help them evaluate and change their priorities and modes of operation where ecumenical commitment demands such a change.

Group 3: On new models of ecumenical sharing

This group chose to reject the term "model" and instead articulated a number of working principles for resource-sharing:

1. All aspects of resource-sharing must be people-centred, that is, applied for the benefit of marginalized and poor people in their struggles for a just and humane society. Of particular importance is the principle of self-reliance for individuals as well as regions. Self-reliance implies that people involved in their struggle for liberation must be the decision-makers of their own affairs; people must have the right to raise financial resources which would be applied to the people's own purposes, especially for their fullest liberation; people must share a vision of people's struggles which unites them in the cause of justice; local initiatives of self-reliance and the building of solidarity links for regional unity must be strengthened.

2. The major contribution of Asia to international resource-sharing may well be the skills and abilities to humanize the institutions and organizations that are necessary tools of human development.

3. The sharing of human resources must take priority, i.e. the exchange of ideas through the exchanging of people with strong links and commitment to people's organizations.

4. It is essential to discover a "new order" of political economics which displays radical changes in those systems under which we are governed.

5. Priority should be given to women to develop and present options in political, economic, social and cultural transformation, for it is clear that the initiatives of women involved in resource-sharing display the originality and freedom of cooperation which characterizes the best of human relationships.

6. Information must be shared which could contribute to the liberation of peoples. It is essential to recognize collaborators in justice from all countries in the world.

7. The rich human resources of Asia must be utilized in the elimination of injustice which could be achieved at minimal costs by establishing a human resource file enabling a bank of human resources which could be made available for local regional needs.

Specific recommendations

1. People-centred, people-oriented:
a) For CCA to facilitate South-South dialogues, exchange of personnel, and engage in other relevant activities among people involved in people's movements. Donor agencies will be challenged to support these efforts.
b) For WCC and CCA to facilitate North-South dialogues, exchange of personnel, and engage in other relevant activities between people involved in people's movements in both North and South for solidarity building. Donor agencies will likewise be challenged and encouraged to support these efforts.
c) For agencies to pay attention to the problems of their own people, and to facilitate the links between third-world action groups based in the first world and action groups involved in third-world struggles.
d) For WCC and agencies to facilitate sharing of information. There is a need to translate pertinent documents coming out of various conferences and consultations to be shared with all people in their own languages.
e) New procedures on accountability means accountability of donor agencies to our people.

2. Towards self-reliance:
a) There has to be extensive research, documentation and study of the concept and principles of self-reliance in terms of people's programmes and finance as soon as possible.
b) We recommend that the CCA institute mechanisms for this by forming a study group composed of people committed to cooperative rather than competitive economic systems and who are committed to the cause of self-reliance as defined above.

CARIBBEAN

In response to the initiative of the office on the Ecumenical Sharing of Resources (ESR) and the Caribbean Conference of Churches (CCC), a meeting was convened in Antigua, West Indies, 17-21 September 1987, to discuss the Caribbean input into the El Escorial conference. It brought together twenty participants comprising Caribbean members of the WCC Central Committee, WCC commissions and other staff, as well as CCC senior staff.

Within the context of the history and evolution of both organizations, certain concerns were identified and prioritized. These centred around the following major questions:

1. How can the Caribbean cooperate with and relate to the WCC holistically when our contacts consist mainly of responses to units and sub-units with seemingly autonomous and unconnected agenda and programmes?
2. How can WCC and CCC work together to help bridge the false dichotomy between mission, development and the search for justice that often characterizes the work of the church?
3. How can the WCC and CCC jointly assist those who see themselves as "donors" or "receivers" to grow in "transparency" and in capacity to realize their own needs as "receivers" based on a searching of the gospel in the concrete context of power and power-sharing?
4. What possibilities are there for the WCC to play an increasing role of moderator and clearing house for the concerns of third-world people and organizations?
5. How can WCC representatives on commissions and the Central Committee who come from the Caribbean become more aware of the concerns of the region in making their input to WCC decision-making bodies?
6. How can the ecumenical movement respond to the ambivalence of local churches which persist in utilizing bilateral channels to the detriment of ecumenical sharing?

In response to these concerns, ways were highlighted in which the Caribbean, considered in many quarters as being "receivers", has been making and continues to make its contributions to ecumenical sharing.

The discussion highlighted contributions made to:

1. Personnel and human resource-sharing — includes recruitment of Caribbean lay and ordained missionaries to serve in Africa and continental Latin America, secondment of top-level religious leadership to world bodies and the ecumenical movement in the North. At the unstructured level is the enormous contribution of immigrant clergy and lay people from the Caribbean to their adopted churches in the North.

2. Educational, moral and cultural sharing — includes religious literature, music, poetry, theology, worship and liturgy, bringing to the world a quality of spirituality and a concrete manifestation of solidarity actions. The Caribbean has provided theological and other opportunities for education for personnel outside the region. We have also shared our unique experience of Roman Catholic-Protestant cooperation.

3. Material sharing — (e.g. financial contributions) to missionary and emergency work in the South, offers of short-term scholarships to the region, the use of the Caribbean as a venue for various consultations in "twinning" in which regional and metropolitan communities are linked.

We feel we can and should offer even more. Such sharing would include the documentation and publicizing of the unique Caribbean experience:

— in the racial religious harmony that we have achieved to a large extent in our communities;
— in our continuing struggle to pursue solidarity with the poor and wholeness of community while giving due regard to the specific needs and concerns which arise out of language, gender, age, race and other differences; and
— in the reality of grassroots ecumenical sharing as the basis for, rather than the consequence of, formal dialogue and institutions.

We could offer as well increased access to Caribbean theological and other educational services and institutions.

In conclusion, we expressed the hope that the El Escorial conference point the way to concrete mechanisms for facilitating and improving ecumenical sharing of resources. In particular, we endorsed the appendix proposals of the draft working document for El Escorial, with special emphasis on the "critical review of present procedures to minimize power and control at the global and regional levels, enhance efficacy and strengthen decision-making at the national/sub-regional level".

We agreed that initiatives for further dialogue between the Caribbean and the WCC with regard to greater cooperation in resource-sharing to the benefit of the poor and local church communities, be pursued as a priority.

EUROPE

A European pre-consultation on resource-sharing was held 1-3 September 1987, in Amersfoort, Netherlands. There were 22 participants, of whom two were women. No youth were able to accept an invitation to attend. General discussion was facilitated by papers from Norway, Sweden and the Netherlands on the state of preparedness within the churches of Eastern and Western Europe to consider the implications of ecumenical resource-sharing for their life and practice.

Discussions took place on the experience of resource-sharing within Europe. In addition to other introductory presentations, Hans Schmocker, secretary for interchurch service of the Conference of European Churches, briefly explained the sharing system through the European resource-sharing group. The main issues raised in the discussion were:

1. The need for the churches of the East and West to strengthen their cooperation in the interests of unity.
2. The need to acknowledge that a great deal of bilateral sharing goes on within Europe on a confessional basis, and that there are a number of ecumenical programmes (e.g. the Churches' Committee on Migration in Europe, the Ecumenical Forum of European Christian Women).
3. The increasing marginalization of more and more groups within our societies and the need to strengthen existing forms and develop new forms of sharing with them.
4. The experience of the European resource-sharing group in its handling of the country programmes for Italy, Spain and Portugal was noted, particularly the action of the three southern European countries in re-drafting a proposed "code of conduct" to govern the mechanisms for the sharing of resources within the format of the country programmes.
5. The need for a renewed commitment of the churches for intra-European sharing.

In group discussion it was recognized that, in the final analysis, European answers had to be found to European problems, such as the lack of spirituality and of community life, racism, refugees and asylum-seekers, unemployment, consumer mentality, militarism. Europeans needed, however, to recognize that they are not sufficient in themselves to attempt to solve these problems. Among the questions pertinent to the ESR discussion that arose were:

1. How can the churches of Europe deepen their contextual analyses and their ability to share insights and experience with one another?
2. In what ways can workers with churches and action groups outside Europe help Europeans where they are blind to important issues in the cultural, social, economic and political fields?
3. With special reference to Western Europe, how can churches from other parts of the world help Europe liberate itself from the individualism and values of the consumer society and rediscover an understanding of "sharing" more consistent with the teaching of the Bible?
4. What does the sharing of resources from Western Europe to the "South" mean in the context of its continuing share in economic domination (as seen in the debt crisis, commodity prices, etc.)?

It was recognized that, at all levels of church life, there was need for a renewal of commitment to "action-based education programmes" designed to move people to involve themselves in issues of injustice between North and South and within Europe itself. The churches need to ask themselves, in an ecumenical spirit:

1. How can the churches and action groups in the South enable us to recognize the priority issues of injustice?
2. In what ways can the churches and other groups in the South enrich the conscientization of the churches and related agencies within Europe?
3. How can the experience of Northern and Southern churches in visitation-exposure programmes be evaluated?
4. How can these experiences help in deciding whether a new ecumenical thrust in promoting such programmes is feasible and desirable?
5. What are the implications for South-South exchange of the articulation of a stronger call from Europe for more North-South and South-North exchanges?

Another group discussion focused on some parts of the working document from the perspective of donor agencies.

Local ecumenical sharing: Local sharing of this sort is fundamental. It is already taking place and is to be encouraged. Where small additional sums of money are needed to facilitate local sharing, it should be made available. The criteria of some agencies do not allow funding of some of these activities (exchanges and visits, solidarity actions, vigils), but others do not have the same constraints and there must be complementarity of action (e.g. between mission boards and development agencies). In addition, donors must be challenged to determine their criteria in the light of the stated needs of churches around the world — not vice versa!

National ecumenical sharing: National bodies, in both South and North, have many important tasks alongside their responsibility for the financial mechanisms of resource-sharing. In all these tasks, including the quest for unity, the emphasis must be on the quality of relationships (as it is in the section on local sharing).

The recommendation asking for openness about bilateral as well as ecumenical relationships applies to both Northern and Southern nations and is a major step. The group endorses the proposal, but whether meetings can be expected to take place annually is a point of debate.

Block grants to national bodies, allowing them to determine their own priorities with the assurance that the funds are available, are to be encouraged, though the questions which arise about the locus of power must continue to be addressed. There is also much disquiet about national bodies which are funded totally from abroad. How can they obtain a significant proportion of local funding? Is there a place for endowment funds in promoting self-reliance?

International ecumenical sharing: Four questions were raised:

1. What is the best role for the WCC? Should it be heavily involved as at present, in the funding process? Is it more important that it be an encourager, facilitator, mediator (someone said "watchdog") of resource-sharing?

2. How can shared decision-making be introduced? Agencies should seek to introduce the principle of mutual accountability and reduce their unilateral control over their funds, as, for example, mission departments which are members of CEVAA or CWM have done. Should the creation of more such communities, or partnerships, be envisaged? (They have the merit of facilitating far more than mere financial sharing: they involve personal relationships, non-material sharing, giving *and* receiving by all, and shared power.) Could some new international partnerships of this sort be established to include churches with no historical Northern partners (e.g. the Orthodox and African independent churches?) And how are such resource-sharing partnerships to relate to the other ecumenical instruments such as national resource-sharing bodies and round-table structures?

3. What are the implications of being, or of refusing to be, channels of government funds? How far may the first option entail compromise and lead to the churches becoming part of a political package deal? How far does the second option mean forfeiting the opportunity of political dialogue? This is a complex conceptual issue that must be examined in Spain from the perspective of ecumenical resource-sharing.

4. How can Christian agencies ensure that they retain their distinctive Christian values as they grow in size, handle a greater volume of funds? How can they ensure that the "professionalism" of staff does not impede good interchurch relationships? It is vital that agencies are open to self-critical reflection and the constructive criticism of partners on this score. It is improper to expect small church project-holders to complete forms which would tax the abilities of large European organizations!

Two further points were discussed:

1. Our understanding of stewardship: There is a malaise in the sharing system which arises from structural constraints and cultural differences. North and South must learn together to interpret God's will in consultation with each other. Sharing theology will give new meaning to the concepts of community and fellowship, and to world mission as a whole.

Stewardship must be seen as a shared responsibility rather than an individual responsibility.

2. Our readiness to enter a commitment: Even after ten years of working at the resource-sharing process, some felt that the Spain consultation is too soon — indeed, it will always be too soon — to commit churches and agencies to an ecumenical discipline. Participants in Spain will have to be completely open about the difficulties which they may expect to meet if a "call to commitment" is made. Yet we affirm that we want to make the changes that an ecumenical discipline will require, and with the help and encouragement of our partners in the South we will take the first steps.

LATIN AMERICA

The consultation on the ecumenical sharing of resources (ESR) in Latin America was held 22-24 April 1987 in Lima, Peru. Three themes were addressed: the biblical and theological basis of ESR; guiding principles of ESR; ESR in local, national and international perspective.

Group 1: Biblical and theological basis

Keeping in mind the 500th anniversary of the European conquest of Latin America, this group reflected on the struggle between the forces of life and anti-life which has marked the history of the continent and which is still going on. The many struggles faced by the people of Latin America were named. In the face of these struggles, it was recognized that signs of the power of life are stirring as more and more people come to an awareness of their own dignity, of their ability and of the need to fight unremittingly for life. This fight takes the form of rediscovering their own cultural values, getting to know the underlying causes of their oppression, and developing organized strength as an instrument in the struggle for the people's demands.

The churches, too, are a part of the struggle, sometimes at the cost of great sacrifice, as they embody the conviction that Jesus Christ is present among the poorest of the poor. This change of heart in sectors of our churches has been based on the deepening of biblical and theological reflection which inspires their action and commitment. Jesus Christ presents us with a model for sharing, which was culminated as he relinquished everything on behalf of people. The death and resurrection of our Lord Jesus Christ are still of the utmost significance for our struggles. This ultimate gift of Jesus is an inspiration to all who suffer and a hope that is reinforced by the promise of the risen Lord who tells that *it will not always be so*. It is this hope which enables us to go on struggling.

Remembering all this, we firmly believe that in its mission today the church must, through the ecumenical sharing of resources, bear witness to an attitude that reaffirms life in the face of the death that is a recurring feature in Latin America and the Caribbean. The act of sharing, when it is done with justice, is a life-giving act which transforms and evangelizes the giver and the receiver. Giving and receiving are not just a question of money. Giving and receiving should be acts which give birth to freedom.

Group 2: Principles and criteria

1. In the ecumenical commitment there is a basic and essential element of sharing with others in critical human situations and in processes of social change.
2. It is essential to arrive at an understanding and common acceptance of the priorities in Latin America and in the third world, bearing in mind that these priorities must be formulated together by all the parties involved in the ecumenical sharing of resources.
3. The ecumenical sharing of resources must be based on the principle of mutual trust founded on mutual criticism.
4. The principle of equality in the process of development or social change is fundamental; that is, the right to make decisions and participate in everything that affects their lives, social context, relations, programmes and methods of working.
5. Equally essential is total solidarity, which means sharing in suffering and the struggle for justice and human welfare.
6. The sharing of the resources we possess is founded on the existence of the ecumenical spirit, where all relationships and results are the fruit of a common effort.
7. The principle of shared responsibility must be respected in resource-sharing. This means that we are all responsible for our national, regional and international situation.
8. The sharing of power is an imperative in resource-sharing. We have to discern the structures of power in our churches and ecumenical organizations, and examine the nature of our decision-making processes.
9. There must be constant critical dialogue among the members and the community of ecumenical resource-sharing.

10. The churches and national, regional and international bodies must know about the underlying causes of injustice in Latin America and the rest of the world so that they can formulate ESR policies which contribute to the process of liberation.

11. Nine points were identified for consideration in the development of criteria and policies for the implementation of the above principles:

    a) the educational dimension of reflection, training and critical study of the realities of our respective situations;

    b) complementarity, which means the sharing of all resources, not only financial;

    c) strengthening of congregations and popular organizations and their participation in all processes;

    d) current processes and relationships must be examined to the end of maximizing the effectiveness and efficiency of ESR;

    e) ESR priorities must be set in terms of local situations which are then related to the global priorities fixed by the ecumenical organizations;

    f) ESR should give priority to support for the churches as they contribute to the search for solutions to the problems of the poor;

    g) the great diversity which exists in the form and content of sharing must be developed further for the improvement of all our exchanges whether they be of information, of support, or of human and financial resources;

    h) the theology of liberation is a contribution to the ESR by the churches and peoples of Latin America which constitutes a substantial input of a non-economic nature;

    i) other resources and initiatives are important, specifically research findings, popular technologies, and exchanges of experiences between the churches and popular groups within Latin America, and should be shared within the ESR process.

Group 3: ESR in local, national and international perspective

This group began by identifying and discussing the shortcomings in the current ESR mechanism and moved on to a discussion of the future prospects of ecumenism, which resulted in three main emphases. The first of these was the challenge posed by the tension existing between the traditional church, whose understanding of the struggle for life is still somewhat immature, and the ecumenical movement, which has reached an understanding that has even led to ecumenism being equated with the defence of life. This should be seen as a creative difference that challenges the ecumenical movement.

A second and related emphasis is that of the twofold task of relating to popular movements and the traditional churches. The ecumenical movement should strengthen support for popular movements and at the same time develop alternatives which will enable it to encourage the traditional churches to move forward in their commitment for life, justice and peace. Of particular importance would be dialogue between the ecumenical bodies and the churches, and the strengthening of the ecumenical movement in countries and regions where it is weak or non-existent.

Finally, the sharing of decision-making in the ESR process was discussed at length. A new, responsible, flexible, non-institutional, dynamic approach is needed where the focus is on quality, not quantity. One alternative which has been passed on to CLACER (the Latin America regional resource-sharing group) with the approval of the present consultation for due study and action proposes regional bodies which would be responsible for fixing strategies, priorities, criteria and policies for sharing, while sub-regional bodies could take charge of the process of analysis and decisions relating to local projects. The importance of determining overall aims for regions, and clear principles to guide decision-making on projects was stressed. The aspect of efficiency on projects was emphasized, including the need for regular evaluations, systematic compilation and summarizing of results, shortcomings, errors and difficulties. The identification of local organizations is important if local people are to be involved in decision-making. There is a need to change the present focus, which stresses administrative and financial aspects, to give more place to pastoral and theological aspects and local priorities. The task of giving continuous support to churches and groups which have made an option for the poor is vital in order to strengthen and encourage them. An up-to-date directory of institutional, human, educational, and technical resources in Latin America and the Caribbean would be a great help. Finally, appropriate strategies to deal with the alarming wave of neo-conservatism that is spreading in Latin America should be drawn up.

Proposal to CLACER: It is proposed that an evaluation be made of the procedures currently being used for ESR in Latin America and the Caribbean, to establish whether the purposes for which CLACER was originally founded are being fulfilled, to identify the weak points in its operation, to devise appropriate and effective mechanisms, and even to establish whether or not the existence of CLACER is justified. This evaluation process should include an initial phase of self-evaluation, and a second phase involving cooperating agencies, churches, ecumenical bodies, etc.

MIDDLE EAST

The enlarged meeting of the Middle East resource-sharing group (MERSC) was held 6-8 April 1987, as a joint meeting of the Middle East Council of Churches (MECC) and the WCC to discuss the regional mechanism for resource-sharing and future partnership of the MECC-WCC, and the input of the Middle East to the world consultation. Three issue areas were identified: local and regional levels of resource-sharing; organization of resource-sharing; and impact of foreign aid. All groups were asked to consider the biblical and theological aspects of resource-sharing.

Group 1: Local and regional level of resource-sharing

This group affirmed the biblical and theological foundation of resource-sharing and called for an intensification of theological reflection on issues related to the region. The eucharist was seen as necessitating sharing with the wider community, sharing which is expressed through the identification and solidarity with the poor and suffering. Resources, gifts and talents are entrusted to us as stewards for Christian service which must embrace the whole human being and the whole of creation.

The need for the identification of real local needs and the mobilization and utilization of local resources was stressed, particularly in relation to long-term visioning and planning, human resource development, participation of people on all levels, maximizing local contributions to foreign aid applications, and encouraging local ecumenical forms of diakonia. The need for awareness-building and conscientization about the sharing of local resources was seen as an important aspect of Christian education. Regular personal contributions at the local level were encouraged to establish self-sufficiency. Projects which can be covered locally, nationally or regionally should be encouraged.

National screening of projects in the region was not seen as being feasible for the time being, although a country programme was recommended as a means to help churches grow together. Round-table structures were viewed with caution. In order to strengthen the diakonia of the churches it was recommended that each church should set up its priorities and formulate its projects on a national (sub-national) level.

Regional-sharing was understood to be restricted to non-material resources. Although in general churches of the region have been recipients as far as material resources are concerned, they may be a source of enrichment to churches outside the region in their struggle for life, existence, justice and peace. It was recommended that proposals for achieving mutuality between regions be worked out at the world conference in October.

Group 2: Organization of resource-sharing

In a preamble to general guidelines for the organization of resource-sharing, this group affirmed a growing expressed commitment on the part of the churches in the Middle East to work together in the MECC towards unity and common participation. However, their situation as minorities in a religiously pluralistic society imposes some limitations on communications and sharing. Moreover, socio-political and religious polarizations and challenges make churches more concerned with the continuity of their presence and witness and the preservation of their particular identities. There is a growing awareness that the privileged form of witness in the religiously pluralistic society is diakonia through sharing in love and humility. The sharing of spiritual and material resources may be an important step towards the realization of Christian community (koinonia) centred in the eucharist. Sharing within the community of faith should also lead to sharing with people of other faiths. The eucharist as the foundation of the spirituality of sharing should be further elaborated and clarified by the international conference in Spain. The historical reality and the theological perceptions of the Middle East churches should be taken very seriously when defining the resource-sharing process in the region as well as through wider partnerships.

Five guiding principles for the organization of a resource-sharing process were identified: (1) spiritual nurture and renewal; (2) ecumenicity as a process towards church unity; (3) human solidarity beyond religious and ethnic boundaries; (4) participation of churches and people concerned in planning and decision-making; (5) diversity of the historical and current realities of the different churches and the common challenge.

This group *recommended* resource-sharing procedures which take into consideration the role of the resource-sharing group, optimum objectivity in evaluation and decision-making, credibility, mutual accountability and efficiency in the exercise of sharing and partnership.

The group discussed in some detail proposed structures of decision-making for resource-sharing projects and programmes, including recom-

mendations regarding pre-screening decisions and the process of decision-making on the national level. Regarding regional decisions, the rich
experience of the existing regional groups based on deep reflection,
participative sharing, and credible decision-making, encourages the continuation of the regional approach. Specific recommendations were
developed for the organization of a regional resource-sharing group.
Functional staff support from the MECC and the resource-sharing staff in
the WCC was recommended to help animate the regional resource-
sharing process.

In regard to international sharing, it was felt that the resource-sharing
situation has been significantly oriented towards material resources, but
has neglected other concerns common to the life and witness of the
churches. Because of the need of the Middle East churches for relations
with mission partners in the search for unity and common witness, and in
order to promote more balanced recognition of the various charismas and
resources available in the ecumenical movement, several *recommendations* were made, including that CWME and other WCC sub-units give
greater attention to the Middle East on their agendas, and that a consultation involving the WCC-MECC and partners from the mission and service
agencies be organized to study the impact of international development in
the Middle East and formulate appropriate ecumenical strategies for
resource-sharing.

Group 3: Impact of foreign aid

This group discussed the differences in resource-sharing in relation to
local churches and para-church organizations. Negative aspects of
resource-sharing through para-church organizations were identified, as
well as negative effects of bilateral sharing within the ecumenical family
structure. Concerns with regard to the ecumenical system included loss of
identity of the smaller churches; historical ties which existed before the
ecumenical system and which cannot be ignored; loss of security of
"mother" churches, alienation and dehumanization when the people
behind the facts and figures tend to be forgotten; dependency on external
resources rather than regional/local resource-sharing; and difficulty of
monitoring of all types of funding.

Non-financial resources which the Middle East churches can share with
the North were identified, including human resources, humaneness, life-
style, family life, spirituality and heritage of Christianity, experience of
minority and suffering churches. Resources which could be shared
regionally or South-South included exchange of experience and expertise;

material resources of hospitality, facilitating transport, etc.; and mutuality of faith, culture and socio-political circumstances.

Recommendation: that an ecumenically-based process is needed to facilitate resource-sharing *in and from the region* which would include: (1) support of the ongoing programmes of the MECC; (2) a study to identify the needs of the churches, particularly the marginalized; (3) an indepth study of the para-church organizations on background, funding, political/ideological ties, motives and impact; (4) guidelines for churches on dealing with the para-church organizations to accompany the study; (5) monitoring all follow-up of external funding through a simple procedure based on trust and not control; (6) an aggressive communications strategy, South-North and regional, to increase the awareness of the richness as well as the plight of the Christians in the region, to counterbalance existing misconceptions and prejudices, and to fill the spiritual vacuum as a need and not as an accommodation in the North presently being exploited by the para-church groups.

PACIFIC

The enlarged meeting of the Pacific Advisory Group (PAG) took place in Suva, Fiji, 27-29 April 1987. Presentations were made on aspects of ecumenical sharing in the Pacific, the involvement of the Pacific churches in mission and development, and the international relationships of the churches, by Mr John Doom (French Polynesia) and Rev. Galuefa Aseta (Western Samoa). Special small group attention was given to three areas: resource-sharing mechanisms for the Pacific, intra-regional sharing, and para-church organizations.

Group 1: Resource-sharing mechanisms for the Pacific

Sharing is understood as a process of mutual giving and receiving between people. Ecumenical resource-sharing, therefore, really means a sharing of material resources, finance, power, decision-making, expertise and so forth locally, nationally and regionally and with the overseas partners as an expression of our oneness in faith and hope, and in our service to our Lord Jesus Christ. Pacific people must participate in decision-making, and accountability must be a mutal process. Because it is difficult for many Pacific people to understand "systems" whereby resources are made available, ways must be found to assist the churches and the national councils of churches to understand the systems of ecumenical sharing and stewardship responsibilities.

Recommendation: that the WCC/CICARWS Pacific desk and the PCC cooperate to facilitate such information-sharing and training which will strengthen the understanding and stewardship involved in sharing resources ecumenically, including developing personnel resources.

It was suggested that the resource-sharing mechanisms be expanded to include four regional sub-groupings in the PAG as well as a PCC general secretary and funding agencies, and that sub-regional relationships with local projects be strengthened. As well, more structured involvement by church leaders, women, youth, NCC and mission boards was recommended.

In light of the principle that power can only be shared if people are allowed to participate, it was *recommended* that programmes be undertaken on the local level to make people understand the structure of the church and power within that structure which could enable people to participate more fully.

Suggestions were made for mechanisms to facilitate the reciprocal sharing of resources (financial as well as personnel, cultural, spiritual, theological, artistic, dramatic, literary) inside and outside the Pacific region. Within the region, team visits between sub-regions were envisioned. The PCC is to arrange sub-regional visitations with the churches in the area, and the WCC the visits with other regions.

To enable some assessment of the wealth of resources within the Pacific churches and how their resources could be shared for the building of the kingdom of God, it was *recommended:*

a) that the PCC prepare a questionnaire to be completed by each church and council of churches; and

b) that the results be collated and shared with Pacific churches and NCCs and that they be encouraged in their ecumenical discussions to seek ways of sharing (e.g. multi-purpose hall, training programmes, communication equipment, libraries, people with specific skills, worship materials, information on issues).

Within the context of ecumenical sharing, the question of relationship of WCC member churches with so-called para-churches and other non-church related funding agencies was discussed. It was strongly *recommended* that churches and NCCs in the Pacific region would relate themselves only to those partners which are part of the ecumenical movement or are truly church-based.

It was agreed that the existing links and bilateral relationships of the Pacific churches should be intensified to promote other aspects of ecumenical sharing (dialogue, consultation, visitation) as being of equal importance as material aid to enable churches in the Northern part of the world to participate directly in the daily struggle of the Pacific churches, and to make them more responsive to the spiritual and other gifts which the Pacific churches have to offer to the rest of the world.

The Pacific Conference of Churches is encouraged to seek and to build up relations with the churches of the North, both east and west.

Group 2: Intra-regional sharing

The Pacific is a region in which ecumenical sharing of resources is of particular relevance. Culturally, sharing is part of the normal way of life within families and between people and groups in mutual relationships. Sharing on an ecumenical basis can draw on and revitalize this cultural pattern, extending it beyond the traditional limits to those usually regarded as strangers. The motivation for doing so comes from a clear understanding that this is part of the Christian response to the gospel, and is an expression of Christian commitment.

Within the Pacific region, it is recognized that both recapturing the cultural practice of sharing and carrying out the Christian commitment to share are essential for peace in the region. The sharing of resources between the peoples of the Pacific can be a way of strengthening the region.

Ecumenical sharing with the Pacific needs to happen at all levels. Only if churches in a local situation respond to the needs of other churches and to those in need regardless of church denomination, faith or culture, can the commitment to sharing at a national and then at a regional level be possible.

It is recognized that Pacific churches are tied into international and bilateral relationships within their denominations, and do not have the habit of sharing with churches of other denominations in their local situation. However, each local church has resources which can be shared with others — with other churches, or together with them in response to local needs. It is suggested that such sharing can begin in a small way, and that local issues such as land questions or natural disasters can be a means of local sharing of resources. In practice, each situation will determine the appropriate starting point.

Four principles are accepted as basic to sharing in the Pacific. First, all groups (and individuals) have needs, and all have something to share.

Second, such sharing can begin now and is possible even at times of scarcity. Third, churches which focus on keeping their resources solely for their own use are poor. Finally, the principle of recognizing that all that is shared is of value can be established at a local level, and ensuring that the resources which are shared nationally, regionally, or outside the region are of value.

Resources of theological and spiritual sharing, as well as material resources which can be shared locally, nationally and regionally were identified. It has been clarified that the ways of sharing spiritual and material resources are different. Spirituality cannot be regarded as a commodity that can be systematized in the same way as material resources. As well, the need for constant dialogue between churches is recognized as basic to the sharing of resources. The cost of travel and the need to overcome language barriers are particular difficulties in communication in the Pacific. There should be a particular concern for small and isolated island nations in all ecumenical sharing in the Pacific. Churches need to share their resources to enable communication to take place so that churches in the region can receive adequate information on issues of concern and share spiritual and material resources with one another.

If requested, external partners should make funds available to PCC specifically for its work of strengthening regional and national sharing. At the local level, recapturing and revitalizing the traditional values of sharing in the local culture, linking these to the Christian commitment for sharing, and using local resources for the development of self-reliance were especially noted. It was also said that instead of "sharing of power" one might rather think in terms of "power of sharing."

Group 3: Para-church organizations

This group began by examining ecumenical sharing in the biblical context affirming that sharing in the eucharist, mission, money, and other forms of ecumenical sharing follow after sharing Christ. This group recommended that a paragraph be added to the working document related to the biblical context to indicate the sinful nature of the world we live in. The struggle between evil and good is a reality of our world. The church has to live and witness in this context. It is the root cause of injustice in everything that we do.

Ecumenical sharing is the basis of our commitment, mission and life. It is not a special department within the structure of our churches. Therefore, ecumenical relationships begin at home, between and among local churches. Old divisions and differences tend to become barriers of ecumenism, so the call to repentance is vitally important as an ongoing part of ecumenism.

The discussion of para-church organizations stressed that the directness and easy availability of aid makes the work of the para-church organizations more appealing for some churches than the ecumenical sharing. But the experiences in some churches which have received this aid have indicated that these aids are harmful to the growth of their churches. We therefore *recommend* that a programme of awareness-raising should be undertaken to inform the Pacific churches about the system, theology, and motives of these groups. It is further *recommended* that with regard to the Pacific churches and their commitment to ecumenical sharing, a participatory approach with all partners should be honoured and respected.

Members of the Planning Group

In July 1985 the Executive Committee of the WCC appointed the following persons to be members of the Planning Group for the World Consultation on Resource Sharing:

Bishop D. J. Ambalavanar, Church of South India, Diocese of Jaffna, Sri Lanka, member of PCR Commission (was elected Moderator by the members of the Planning Group)

Rev. Israel Batista Guerra, Methodist Church in Cuba, member of CCPD Commission (became CCPD staff member in January 1987)

Mrs Imogene Collins, Executive Secretary, Liberian Council of Churches

Dr James A. Cogswell, Director, Division of Overseas Ministries, National Council of Churches of Christ in the USA

Rev. Warner Conring, Director Church Development Service, Evangelical Church of Germany, member of CICARWS Commission

Mrs Rosangela Jarjour, Ayia Napa Conference Centre Cyprus, National Evangelical Synod of Syria and Lebanon, member of Central Committee and CWME Commission

Dr Armando Luza Salazar, Methodist Church of Peru, ULAJE (Union of Latin American Ecumenical Youth)

Bishop Nifon Ploiesteanul, Patriarchal Assistant, Orthodox Church of Rumania, member of CICARWS Commission

Rev. Dr A. George Ninan, Associate General Secretary, Christian Conference of Asia

Mrs Margaretha Ringström, Study Secretary, Church of Sweden Mission

List of Participants

Delegates and fraternal delegates

Father Georges Abouzakhm, Greek Orthodox Patriarchate of Antioch and All East, Syria (CCPD)

Pastor Carmelo Alvarez, Departamento Ecuménico de Investigaciones, Costa Rica

Mr James C. A. Ameda, Church of Uganda

Rev. Ayakana-Komla Amouzou, Evangelical Church of Togo

Mr Robert Anderson, United Church of Canada

Rev. Leonardo Alfred Appies, South Africa (Urban Rural Mission)

Ms Noris Araque de Maldonado, Latin American Council of Churches, Ecuador

Metropolitan Thomas Mar Athanasios Episcopal, Orthodox Syrian Church Catholicate of the East (India)

Rev. Dr John S. Barton, Anglican Church of Canada

Mr Bena-Silu, Kimbanguist Church Zaire

Rev. René Bideaux, United Methodist Church USA

Ms Peggy Billings, United Methodist Church USA

Dr Dale Bisnauth, Caribbean Conference of Churches (Guyana)

Ms Sandra M. Blamey, Australian Council of Churches

Rev. Drs Bert Boer, Netherlands Reformed Church

Ms Susan M. Brook, Evangelical Lutheran Church in America

Ms Caroline Brown, Anglican Church of Canada

Dr Katheryn M. Brown, African Methodist Episcopal Church, USA

Mr Marc Brunschweiler, CIMADE, France

Rev. Manuel Pedro Silva Cardoso, Portuguese Council of Christian Churches

Ms Selma T. Chipenda-Dansokho, Senegal, Youth

Dr James A. Cogswell, National Council of Churches of Christ in the USA

Ms Imogene Collins, Liberian Council of Churches

Rev. Warner Conring, Evangelical Church in Germany, EKD

Ms Friederike Costa, Bund der Evangelischen Kirchen der DDR, Youth

Prof. Enrique Mario Dabala, Iglesia Valdense - Río de la Plata, Uruguay

Ms Jean Davidson, Presbyterian Church in Canada
Bishop Din Dayal, Church of North India
Ms Afaf Deeb-Kandis, Middle East Council of Churches, Cyprus (Lebanon)
Ms Dorothy Devine, Scottish Churches Action for Development, Papua New
　　Guinea, Youth
Rev. Dr Zwinglio M. Dias, CEDI, Brazil (Urban Rural Mission)
Ms María E. Díaz, Chili, Youth
Rev. Otto Dilger, Evangelical Mission Southwest Germany (EMS)
Rev. Roland A. H. Dumartheray, Swiss Missionary Council
Ms Iman Mariam Ekdawi, Coptic Orthodox Church, Egypt, Youth
Ms Nashilongo Elago, Council of Churches in Namibia
Rev. Karl-Axel Elmquist, Diakonia, Sweden
Mr Jan A. Erichsen, Church of Norway, NCA
Rt Rev. Maitland M. Evans, United Church of Jamaica and Grand Cayman
Mr Pascal Fabre, DEFAP, France
Ms Nimalka Fernando, Sri Lanka (Sub-unit on Women)
Mr Laitia Fifita, Tonga National Council of Churches
Mr Walid Sami Geraisy, Middle East Council of Churches, Youth
Ms Judith Gillespie, Episcopal Church USA
Rev. Orestes Gonzalez Cruz, Consejo Ecuménico de Cuba
Mr Claudio E. Gonzalez Urbina, FASIC, Chile
Rev. Wm E. Gorski, Evangelical Lutheran Church in Chile
Dr Wolf-Dieter Graewe, Bund der Evangelischen Kirchen in der DDR
Ms Pamela H. Gruber, Moderator CICARWS (UK)
Mr Ilustre Z. Guloy, National Council of Churches in the Philippines
Ms Anita Häussermann, Evangelical Church in Germany
Mr Mats Hermansson, Church of Sweden, Youth
Mr Helmut Hertel, Dienste in Uebersee, FRG
Mr Eimart van Herwijnen, Dutch Interchurch Aid
Dr Gerard van der Horst, ICCO (NL)
Dr John O. Humbert, Christian Church (Disciples of Christ) in the USA and
　　Canada
Metropolitan G. Yohanna Ibrahim, Syrian Orthodox Church of Antioch and all
　　the East (Syria)
Ms Rosangela Jarjour, Evangelical Synod of Syria and Lebanon (Syria)
Rev. Riad Jarjour, Middle East Council of Churches (Cyprus)
Drs Magritha B. Jongeneel-Touw, Netherlands Missionary Council
Mr Juan Francisco Juarez Zapata, Baptist Convention of Nicaragua
Bishop Samir Kafity, Episcopal Church in Jerusalem and the Middle East
　　(CICARWS)
Ms Wilhelmina J. Kalu, Nigeria (Education)
Mr Kang Moon-Kyu, Korea (CICARWS)
Mr Dismas Karasi, Uganda Voluntary Work Camps Association, Youth
Ms Henriette Marianne Katoppo, PTE/Asia, Indonesia

Ms Sarah K. Kemoli, All Africa Conference of Churches (Kenya)
Ms Anne Kerepia, Papua New Guinea (CICARWS)
Mr Prawate Khid-Arn, Asia Regional Fellowship, Thailand (CCPD)
Ms Jacqueline King, Caribbean Conference of Churches (Barbados)
Dr W. Kistner, South African Council of Churches
Mr Reiner Klare, Bread for the World, FRG
Rev. Josateki Fifi Koroi, Methodist Church in Fiji
Rev. Gyula Kovats, Reformed Church of Romania
Rev. M. M. Kuchera, Zimbabwe Christian Council
Rev. Adam Kuczma, Conference of European Churches (Poland)
Mr Adil Kudsi, Orthodox Youth Movement (Cyprus)
Ms Prema Doss Kumari, India (Programme to Combat Racism)
Mr Kwon Dal Hyun, Presbyterian Church of Korea
Rev. Kwon Ho-Kyung, Hong Kong, Korea (Urban Rural Mission)
Mr Yin-Cho Philip Lam, Hong Kong Christian Council
Rev. Thorkild Schousboe Laursen, Danish Missionary Council
Rev. J. Brian Lee, Uniting Church in Australia
Ms Renée Lee, Malaysia
Rev. Sakari Lehmuskallio, Evangelical Lutheran Church of Finland
Mr Roberto Lemaitre, DEI, Costa Rica, Youth
Ms Yvonne Lin Mei-Jung, Taiwan, Youth
Rev. Isaac E. Makanta, Evangelical Lutheran Church in Tanzania
Mr Kosti Yekonia Manibe, Sudan Council of Churches
Mr Friedrich Manske, Prot. Association for Cooperation Development (EZE), FRG
Rev. Pakoa B. Maraki, Presbyterian Church of Vanuatu
Ms Erika Märke, EZE/AGKED Women's network, FRG
Ms Emma Mashinini, South African Council of Churches
Mr Patrick A. Matsikenyiri, Zimbabwe (Renewal and Congregational Life)
Rev. Suguru Matsuki, National Christian Council in Japan
Sister Mary McAleese, UK (Urban Rural Mission)
Bishop Keith A. McMillan, Anglican Province of the West Indies, Belize
Rev. Sandor Merétey, Ecumenical Council in Hungary
Ms Catherine Metzner, France, Youth
Mr Bento Eliseu Michangula, Anglican Church of Mozambique
Ms Peggy Reiff Miller, Church of the Brethren, USA
Rev. Tadashi Mitsui, Canada (CICARWS)
Rev. Hans-Martin Moderow, Bund der Evangelischen Kirchen in der DDR
Ms Jeanne Moffat, United Church of Canada
Mr Sione K. F. Motuahala, Pacific Conference of Churches, Fiji (Tonga)
Rev. John C. Moyer, USA (Urban Rural Mission)
Ms Theresa Moyo, Zimbabwe (CCPD)
Ms N. Mary Mxadana, South Africa (CICARWS)
Ms Maud Nahas, Lebanon (CICARWS)

Bishop Mihaita Nifon, Romanian Orthodox Church
Rev. A. George Ninan, Christian Conference of Asia, Japan (India)
Bishop George M. Njuguna, The Church of the Province of Kenya
Mr Elisha R. Q. Nkoka, Lesotho, Youth
Rev. Nyansako-ni Nku, Presbyterian Church in Cameroon
Rev. Dr Zablon Nthamburi, Methodist Church in Kenya
Ms Muena-Kalenda Nzeba Kalombo, Eglise du Christ au Zaire
Mr Carlos Ocampo, Ecumenical Centre for Development, Philippines (CCPD)
Prof. Duane A. Olson, Evangelical Lutheran Church in America
Rev. Kenichi Otsu, Christian Conference of Asia (Japan)
Rev. Hans Ott, Brot für Brüder, Switzerland
Ms Seta Panboukian, Armenian Orthodox Church, Lebanon
Mr Ralph A. Pannett, Council for Mission and Ecumenical Cooperation, New
    Zealand
Ms Mine Pase, Pacific Conference of Churches, American Samoa
Rev. Sophie I. Patty, Evangelical Christian Church in Irian Jaya, Indonesia
Bishop M. Elia Peter, Methodist Church in India
Rt Rev. Dr P. Victor Premasagar, Church of South India
Rev. John Ralph Pritchard, Methodist Church, UK
Dr Christopher Radim Pulec, Czechoslovakia, Youth
Drs A. Quashie, Partnership for World Mission, UK
Ms A. Birgitta Rantakari, Evangelical Lutheran Church of Finland
Ms Vaosoa Ravalomanana, Church of Jesus Christ in Madagascar
Ms Margaretha Ringström, Church of Sweden Mission
Mr Timothy Michael Robinson, Church of England
Rev. Claudia Roehrig, Yugoslavia (CICARWS)
Rev. Dr Wilhelmus A. Roeroe, Christian Evangelical Church in Minahasa,
    Indonesia
Ms Eliana Rolemberg, CESE, Brazil (CCPD)
Rev. Bernhard Rui, Evangelical Church of Lutheran Confession in Brazil
Mr Fructuoso Sabug Jr, Philippines, Youth
Ms Shashi Sail, India (CICARWS)
Mr Nabil Samuel Abadir, Coptic Evangelical Church, Egypt
Bishop Arturo Sánchez Galán, Spanish Reformed Episcopal Church
Mr Juan Schaad, Evangelical Church of the River Plate
Mr Hans Ernst Schmocker, Conference of European Churches (Switzerland)
Mr Johan Hendrik Schravesande, Reformed Churches in the Netherlands
Mr Juan A. Schvindt, Latin American Council of Churches, Brazil
Mr Narciso Sepúlveda Barra, Pentecostal Church Mission
Bishop Serapion, Coptic Orthodox Church, Egypt
Ms Colleen Shannon, Presbyterian Church USA
Rev. Gordon Shaw, British Council of Churches
Mr Humberto Martín Shikiya, Evangelical Methodist Church of Argentina
Rev. Orlando Silva, Evangelical Pentecostal Church, Brazil

Rev. O.P.T. Simorangkir, Batak Protestant Christian Church, Indonesia
Mr Rajan S. Singh, Hong Kong, India (Urban Rural Mission)
Ms Keresi Roro Sinusetaki, Fiji, Youth
Rev. Johan Skjortnes, Norwegian Missionary Society
Mr Lennart Skov-Hansen, Danchurchaid, Denmark
Bishop Olafur Skulason, Icelandic National (Lutheran) Church
Mr Enilson Rocha Souza, Brazil (CICARWS)
Rev. Barbara Jean Stephens, National Council of Churches in New Zealand
Rev. Pierre Strauss, Swiss Interchurch Aid
Dr Bert A. Supit, Indonesia (Christian Medical Commission)
Ms Mushira Tawfik Tadros, Egypt, Youth
Rev. Larry D. Tankersley, National Council of Churches of Christ in the USA
Ms Connie Tarasar, Orthodox Church in America
Ms Amaal Tawfek, Egypt (Sub-unit on Women)
Rev. Michael H. Taylor, Christian Aid, UK
Rev. Remuna Tufariua, Evangelical Church of French Polynesia, Tahiti
Dr Tom Tuma, Church of Uganda
Ms Patricia Gill Turner, USA (Programme to Combat Racism)
Rev. Dr Fridolin Ukur, Communion of Churches in Indonesia
Bishop Rogers O. Uwadi, Methodist Church of Nigeria
Mr Knud Vad, Denmark, Youth
Rev. Lloyd Gordon Van Vactor, United Church of Christ, USA
Prof. Prócoro Velasques, Brazil (Programme on Theological Education)
Mr Roger Velásquez, CEPAD, Nicaragua
Prof. Daniel Vidal Regaliza, Evangelical Church of Spain
Rev. Barbro K. A.-M. Westlund, Church of Sweden Aid
Mr Dana Wheeler, USA, Youth
Rev. Dr John Christopher Wigglesworth, Church of Scotland
Dr Donald J. Wilson, Presbyterian Church USA
Dr Frederick Russell Wilson, Presbyterian Church USA
Ato Megersa Yadeta, Ethiopian Evangelical Church Mekane Yesus
Rev. Yang Chi-Shou, Presbyterian Church in Taiwan
Mr Seifu Michael Zelleke, All Africa Conference of Churches

Observers

Ms Carol G. Abel, Ecumenical Forum of European Christian Women, UK
Mr Samuel Akle, CEVAA, France (Benin)
Ms Patricia A. Bays, Anglican Consultative Council, Canada
Rev. John Boonstra, Frontier Internship in Mission, Switzerland (USA)
Mr Douglas V. Brunson, Ecumenical Development Cooperative Society (EDCS), Netherlands (USA)
Fr Felipe Duque Sánchez, Episcopal Conference of Spain
Mr Dennis Wayne Frado, Lutheran World Federation, Switzerland (USA)

Mr Hugo García, Ecumenical Movement for Human Rights, Argentina
Fr P.J.E. Gordijn, Misereor, FRG
Mr Graeme Spence Irvine, World Vision International, Switzerland (USA)
Ms Christine Ledger, World Student Christian Federation, Switzerland (Australia)
Ms Mandy Nogarede, World Young Women's Christian Association, Switzerland (UK)
Fr Michel Schooyans, Vatican, Belgium
Mr Emile Stricker, World Alliance of Young Men's Christian Associations, Switzerland
Ms Ted L.E. Strop-von Meyenfeldt, Support Associations EDCS, Netherlands
Rev. Carlos A. Valle, World Association of Christian Communication, UK (Argentina)
Rev. Robert J. Vitillo, Caritas Internationalis (Vatican)

Resource persons

Ms Brigalia Bam, South Africa
Rev. Dr Christopher Duraisingh,
  India/UK
Ms Sithembiso Nyoni, Zimbabwe
Rev. Dr Konrad Raiser, FRG
Ms June Rodriguez, Philippines
Mr Pablo Sosa, Argentina
Ms Jean Zaru, West Bank

WCC staff

Rev. S. Wesley Ariarajah
Mr Israel Batista Guerra
Mr Huibert van Beek
Ms Midge Beguin-Austin
Ms Sylvie Breu-Peter
Ms Patricia Bruschweiler
Mr Théo Buss
Rev. Dr Emilio Castro
Ms Diana Chabloz
Ms Nora Chase
Mr Patrick Coïdan
Ms Maryse Courvoisier
Rev. Kenith David
Ms Pilar Delaraye
Ms Rosemarie Dönch
Mr Michael Dominguez
Ms Nicole Fischer
Ms Marlies Freidig

Ms Shelagh Friedli
Ms Yasmina Gay
Ms Marie-Louise Gehler
Ms María Rosa Giovannini
Ms Elisabeth Gouël
Rev. James Greig
Ms Erna Haller
Dr Irene Heyartz Wagner
Mr Samuel Isaac
Ms Lynda Katsuno
Ms Cornelia Kerkhoff
Ms Monique McClellan
Ms Joyce McNulty
Mr Daniel Moreillon
Ms Malle Niilus
Ms Marta Palma
Ms María Julia Pascual
Rev. Clifford Payne

Ms Lise Phillips
Rev. John Pobee
Dr Klaus Poser
Dr Ghassan Rubeiz
Ms Birgitta Rubenson
Ms Françoise Ruiz

Ms Renate Sbeghen
Ms Jeane Sindab
Ms Thelma Skiller
Ms Ruth Sovik
Dr Eugene Stockwell
Mr Peter Williams

Consultant

Dr Kees van der Poort, Netherlands

Co-opted staff

Mr Antonio Alvarez-Gazapo
Ms Manuela Brown
Ms Rosa Elena Cervantes
Ms Martine Cullot
Ms Christiane Demont
Ms Renate Drewes-Siebel
Ms Erika Ernst
Ms Ursula Gassmann
Ms Ann Goslin
Mr Michel Hourst

Ms Christine Mear
Mr Mike Nahhal
Dr William Nottingham
Mr Luis Odell
Ms María Blanca Peral
Ms Daphne S. de Plou
Ms Anita Richterich
Ms Anne-Lise Robertson
Ms Renate Strecker

Stewards

Ms K. M. Bamwoze, Kenya
Mr Canuto Nkulu Bayeme,
    Spain (Equatorial Guinea)
Mr Fernando Benito, Spain
Mr Alex Buckley, Spain (USA)
Ms Jordi Pallas Capó, Spain
Ms Judit Pallas Capó, Spain
Mr Joaquín García Carbonell, Spain
Mr Alejandro Gómez Menchón, Spain
Mr Juan Marcos Gómez Heras, Spain
Mr Douglas Hartshorne, USA
Mr Joseph Majd Kassab, Lebanon

Ms Beatriz H. Mendoza Gómez, Spain
Ms Sara Moreno García, Spain
Mr Ricardo Moreno García, Spain
Ms Raquel Narciso y Miranda, Spain
Ms Jill Ogilvie, UK
Ms Noemí Poncela, Spain
Mr Miguel Romo, USA
Ms Susana Vidal Roselló, Spain
Mr Alberto Salgado Saco, Spain
Mr Daniel Vergara Muñoz, Spain
Ms Bettina Zöckler, Spain (FRG)

Visitors

Mrs Lynda Frado
Mrs John Humbert
Mrs Frances Irvine
Mrs Cynthia Veronica McMillan

Mrs Barbara Shaw
Mrs Ebba Skulason
Mrs Elba Valle
Mrs Maria van Beek

Acknowledgments

Page vi: "A Hymn on Empty Hands", words by Fred Kaan, music by Rieke Boerma; © words Oxford University Press, London (world, exclusive of USA and Canada); USA and Canada, Hope Publishing Co., Carol Stream, Illinois, USA. Reprinted with permission.

Page 2: "Nkosi, nkosi", music by G. M. Kolisi, from *Freedom is Coming: Songs of Protest and Praise from South Africa*, ed. by Anders Nyberg, 1984 Utryck, Uppsala, Sweden, with the Church of Sweden Mission.

Page 78: "Break Down the Walls", by Fred Kaan and Peter Janssens, © Peter Janssens Musik Verlag, Telgte, Federal Republic of Germany. Reprinted with permission.

Page 90: Russian Orthodox liturgy.